Ackowledgements

Thank you to everyone who gives me advice and encouragement—-

Thank you to Jim Gelarden, my ever-patient husband, for continuing to believe in me through every new nightmare and crisis.

Thank you to my Gram, Katheryn Lynch, for her continuing support and inspiration, and for passing on to me her love of millinery.

Thank you to Marie, whose last name I am embarrassed to say is long forgotten, but who taught me most of what I know about bridal millinery.

Thank you to Barry Bradley (Curator) and Bern 1905 (Assistant Curator), of the Western Reserve Historical Society's Chisholm Halle Costume Wing, for their detailed information on textile care and preservation.

Thank you to Wendy Ulaszewski and Michele Pigza for their wonderful illustrations and graphic design assistance, and especially to Ellen Lynch for making the book look so fabulous.

Thank you to my four editors, Lynn Lunoe, Christine Dougherty, Jennifer Presot, and Jim Gelarden, for finding everything that was wrong with the first few drafts, and especially for finding everything that was right.

Thank you to my family and friends, who — sight unseen — knew this book would be the greatest thing anybody had ever done.

THIS BOOK IS DEDICATED TO MY INCREDIBLE SISTER ELLEN, FOR RESCUING ME AND MAKING IT ALL LOOK SO EASY.

"I Do" Veils

Veils

—SO CAN YOU!

A Step-by-Step Guide
to Making Bridal Headpieces,
Hats and Veils
with Professional Results

CLAUDIA LYNCH

HARPAGON PRODUCTIONS

"I DO" VEILS
—SO CAN YOU!
A Step-by-Step Guide to Making Bridal Headpieces,
Hats and Veils with Professional Results

Claudia Lynch

Harpagon Productions
P.O. Box 161125
Rocky River, Ohio 44116

(216) 333-3143 Phone/Fax

Harpagon Productions is a division of Sideline Design

Illustration by Wendy Ulaszewski, Michele Pigza, and Claudia Lynch
Graphic Design by Michele Pigza/MPDesign and Ellen Lynch/ID.esign
Cover Photography by Wetzler's Studio, Inc.

This book is typeset in Times Roman, Balmoral, Garamond, and Gil Sans.

ISBN Number 0-9650813-6-2

Printed in USA

HARPAGON
PRODUCTIONS

TABLE OF CONTENTS

GETTING STARTED

If you can thread a needle and plug in a glue gun, you can make your own exquisite bridal headpiece.

No kidding — It's really that easy. And although knowing your way around a sewing machine is useful for some techniques — veil edgings, for example — even those techniques are easy to master with just a little practice. Or, perhaps you could get your mother or your cousin or your best friend to help — Surely they'd all be thrilled to be invited to assist in the creation of something this luscious!

How to Use this Book

"I Do" Veils is the first comprehensive written manual for bridal headpiece construction. Before now, professional and amateur headpiece makers developed techniques largely independently of each other. What little information was shared was passed along almost in the manner of folklore or verbal storytelling.

In an effort to keep your own creativity unshackled and to insure that your headpiece will be unique, "I DO" VEILS is not a "project book". Rather, it has been designed as a manual of all of the bridal headpiece techniques used by professional milliners. You will be able to mix and match elements from several different sections of the book to create your own unique design.

It's a good idea to skim through the entire book before you get started, so you'll be familiar with its layout — knowing where to quickly refer for information as you develop your design and construct your headpiece will make the process speedy and enjoyable. Familiarizing yourself with the basic techniques of bridal millinery will give you the confidence to creatively modify those established techniques as your individual headpiece requires.

BE CREATIVE AND TRUST YOURSELF!

Bridal millinery is a form of sculpture, an art rather than a science.

Much of the process of making a bridal headpiece is necessarily makeshift, even for professional milliners. Just because you haven't seen or been taught a particular method does not make it wrong or slipshod work. It probably just means that you've come up with a design so unique and wonderful that it requires its own kind of techniques to bring it to reality!

So if you need a peculiar technique to accommodate your own unique design — something so special it hasn't been covered in "I DO" VEILS — feel free to invent something and use it with great authority and confidence. Sometimes the most inventive millinery designs and solutions actually come from novices to the craft because they are working intuitively, and often an "impossible" problem can be solved ONLY by someone who is not hindered by knowing the "correct" way of solving it!

As long as your headpiece stays together securely and looks wonderful, you've engineered an instantly acceptable millinery method.

HOW MUCH TIME SHOULD I PLAN TO SPEND?

Each headpiece is an individual sculpture. Sculpture is art, and art takes time to produce, so your bridal headpiece is probably not a project to be started an hour before the rehearsal dinner!

The actual time your headpiece will take depends upon so many factors that it's impossible to say exactly how much time you will spend on yours. The headpiece style that you select, the level of your experience, the ornateness or simplicity of your design, how much of a perfectionist you are, and how quickly you work and make decisions are all variables that cannot be broken down into hours and minutes.

If possible, start your headpiece several weeks or even months before your wedding. That will give you plenty of time to work on it at your leisure without having to rush. Perhaps more importantly, it will give you time to walk away from it every so often — If you do that, you'll be able to see it much more clearly when you return, and any design or construction problem that might have caused you to put it aside will seem easily solvable when you come back to it.

How did I do that???

Even if you think you will only be making one headpiece, you'll want to keep a sample of any unusual techniques, to save time in case you ever want to duplicate them. Label the samples with the exact settings for your particular sewing machine (stitch length and width, needle position, etc.), or any other information you think you might forget over time. Who knows — after seeing the professional job you've done on your own headpiece, your friends and relatives may turn to you as their personal bridal headpiece designer!

You're the Designer

Don't let the job title intimidate you — You've been a designer all your life.

If you think you've never designed anything before, take a good look around you — You coordinated the outfit you're wearing today, and selected your hair style. Possibly you helped to choose and arrange the furniture in the room you're sitting in. You know how to set a table, trim a Christmas tree, and wrap a gift.

Okay, so you have selecting, coordinating, and arranging experience — What luck! Those are absolutely all the skills you need to be a bridal headpiece designer. Design is really nothing more than deciding what something is going to look like when it's finished. You don't have to know how to draw, and you can make all the changes you want as you go along, so relax and have a good time!

Getting Started

Have you ever noticed that all fun projects start with a shopping trip?

Go to any bookstore, grocery, or drug store, and pick up a few of the current bridal magazines — *Modern Bride, Bride's, Elegant Bride, Wedding Dresses,* and *Bridal Guide* are available almost everywhere, and you may find even more to choose from. Flipping through the bridal magazines is a fun and easy way to become acquainted with the possibilities, and to get your creative juices flowing.

Visit fabric stores, craft supply stores, or millinery suppliers in your area to get a good idea of the types of frames and trimmings that are available, or send for some of the catalogs in the RESOURCES section at the back of this book. Some of the catalogs also feature finished headpiece designs, which can usually be made from the components in that particular catalog.

Attending bridal fairs and fashion shows is a perfect opportunity to see headpieces displayed on live models. At a fashion show, it is easy to get a sense of which headpiece styles complement a particular gown or hairstyle. It is important to observe not only how a headpiece looks but how easy it is to wear and how securely it remains fastened to the bride's head.

Of course, there is no substitute for experimenting with different shapes and styles on your very own head. Ask to try on the headpieces your friends and family have worn, and check out the selection at millinery suppliers and bridal salons in your area.

Take along a picture of your gown, as well as fabric and lace samples, if you have them. Tuck a few bobby pins into your purse, so you can experiment with a hair style that might work with a headpiece that you like. And as soon as you leave the bridal salon, take notes and draw rough sketches of shapes and trimmings that appeal to you while they are still fresh in your mind.

Be aware that bridal salon salespersons may not be keen to assist you if they know you're there to try on headpieces looking for designs to copy. They would prefer to make a sale, and they might not have the foresight to look upon this as a sales opportunity rather than a waste of their time. So to avoid unnecessary rudeness, go disguised as a potential paying customer. Don't feel guilty about it — After all, if you find the perfect headpiece in their shop, you might conceivably purchase it there instead of going forward with making it yourself.

If you are planning to wear a vintage gown, it is a good idea to do some historical research to determine which headpiece styles were popular at the time your gown was originally made. If the gown belonged to your mother or another family member, ask to see the photographs from her wedding. Your local historical society can also help you find pictures of period weddings, and you may even find copies of bridal magazines from your gown's era at an antique shop or used book store. Feel free to adapt a contemporary headpiece style to wear with your vintage gown, or to update a vintage shape with modern trimmings.

INDING YOUR PERFECT STYLE

If choosing a headpiece to complement your gown were the only consideration, it would be a more straightforward and stress-free task.

Instead, the headpiece must also flatter your size, carriage, personality, hairstyle, and the shape of your head and face. A headpiece must be in correct proportion to your height, and might even take the groom's height into consideration. And, of course, it must appeal to your personal taste and make you feel absolutely wonderful!

As you try them on, notice how different headpiece styles seem to bring out the sparkle in your eyes — or the wort on your nose. Reject the unflattering styles, and look for the ones that compliment all of your best features.

Regardless of its size, your headpiece should be light in weight and light in appearance, so as not to overpower you or your gown. If it looks like the hat is wearing you, scale it down in size or start whittling away the excess trimmings.

Select the size of a headpiece relative to your own proportions. Your headpiece should not make you look too tall or too short or too fat or too thin. A huge picture hat on a very short bride or a tiny pillbox hat worn by a plus-size bride, for example, would both seem out of scale (perhaps they should trade!). A too-tall tiara is problematic for almost everyone — It makes a tall, angular bride appear

If you want to look a little taller, choose a well-proportioned tiara or crown. You can even add a small tiara effect to another headpiece shape to increase the illusion of height. If your groom is close to your height or shorter, consider a Juliet cap, headband, or a cascade of flowers worn at the back of your head — These will add little or no height at all.

As you try on different headpiece styles, try to picture yourself in two of your wedding photographs — The first one is just you as the bride, with your gown, your hair style, your makeup, and your headpiece all perfectly coordinated. The second mental photograph should be of you AT your wedding. Does the picture of you belong at the wedding you've envisioned, and will the headpiece be comfortable enough to wear throughout the day that you've planned? For example, if your reception is to be an outdoor barbecue, a flower wreath (or even a cowboy hat!) with a detachable veil might be a better choice than an elaborately beaded tiara.

Let your headpiece choice reflect your personality as well as the style of the wedding. If you live in blue jeans, and putting on a dress at all makes you feel itchy, choose a sim-

ple, weightless barrette or comb with a small cluster of delicate silk flowers rather than a showy cascade with an excess of pearl leaves and orchids. For a real "girly girl", used to wearing ruffles, lace, curls, and nail polish, a floral wreath or V-band replete with pearl sprays and baby's breath is more appropriate than a plain tailored headband. A bride with a flamboyant, outgoing personality can easily carry a large hat or headpiece that would seem out of proportion on a more reserved bride.

Your ideal design may be symmetrical — that is, exactly the same from side to side — or asymmetrical. Examples of an asymmetrical design are a single rose placed at the side of a cocktail hat, or an arrangement of flowers, pearls, and ribbons located entirely on one side of a V-band. Most headpieces are symmetrical,

taller, and a short bride appear even shorter. If your face is large, you can handle a dramatic asymmetrical arrangement of flowers close to your face, while a bride with more delicate features would be eclipsed by it. A headpiece that is primarily horizontal, like a V-band or a halo, may tend to make you look wider.

but an asymmetrical design can be stunningly spectacular, drawing attention away from your gown and directing it to your face and hair style instead.

Ideally, it should appear that your gown and your headpiece were designed as a coordinating two-piece ensemble. The color, texture, and character of the trimmings should match or blend with the gown, and the colors must be an exact match. (To specify "white" or "ivory" is not sufficient due to the variations within those color families — Use a swatch of the gown fabric as a reference when choosing headpiece materials).Keep these considerations in mind as you choose the shape, size, and decoration of the headpiece, and the resulting design cannot help but be the perfect one for you. If a hard-and-fast rule of thumb would make you feel more confident, here it is — "Frame the face, don't hide it; complement the gown, don't fight it".

WHAT ABOUT MY HAIR?

You're on a roll now, so choose a hair style based on the same considerations you used when designing your headpiece — Proportion, personality, comfort, the style of your gown and headpiece, and the formality of the wedding.

The only other variables are your hair's length, texture, and degree of body or curl. If styling your own hair is among your many talents, or if the style you choose is similar to the one you wear every day, you might decide to style it yourself, but most brides decide to entrust their hair to a professional stylist on the day of the wedding.

Go back through the same stack of magazines you bought when you were still searching for a headpiece design, and look for models who are wearing headpieces similar to yours. Very likely, you will be surprised to find that your headpiece shape seems to work well with a variety of hair styles. Tear out the pictures you like and take them to the hair stylist with you.

Also take your headpiece with you to the styling salon, for both the consultation (if you have one) and the final styling. Your hair style can be designed to work beautifully with your headpiece only if the stylist can see the entire picture. You may even wish to have him or her fasten the headpiece in place for you, insuring that it is positioned correctly and securely.

Remind the hair stylist to avoid spraying any hair spray directly at the headpiece, as it may discolor the fab-

rics or other components over time. Remember — This headpiece is an heirloom!

MAKE A PROTOTYPE

Once you have a design in mind, gather the materials you need for your headpiece and make, as it is called in the trade, a "mockup".

Read through the section of the book that gives the directions for your particular headpiece shape. Use jewelry wire, pins, or floral tape to temporarily hold your components together just well enough to allow you to see if what you've got is what you envisioned. Add, delete, or rearrange the components until you are satisfied with the design.

If your design is a hat, the prototype can be done before or after the frame has been covered in fabric.

Before you take the mockup apart, take photographs of it from several angles. Or, do a quick schematic drawing of your design — use different geometric shapes to represent the components, and label or color-code each component as well. That way, you will have the photographs or drawings to refer to as you complete your headpiece.

GLUE IS PERMANENT!

Just as you would baste the seams first when sewing a dress to allow for fitting and design changes without ruining the materials, pin, baste, or tape the components together so that you can reposition them at will. Be certain of the final design of your headpiece before you begin gluing, and remove the pins one at a time as you glue the trimmings in place.

Most trimmings are applied to the headpiece with hot glue. As a rule of thumb, feel free to hot glue any components that are large enough and opaque enough to hide the glue application completely. Use a white flexible glue instead for lace, pearls, and any other material that might be ruined by hot glue or where the glue might show through or around the component.

Materials & Supplies

A delicate froth of silk flowers, ribbons, and illusion, a bridal headpiece looks fragile enough to be reduced to scraps by an imperceptible breath of wind. Don't let that delicate facade deceive you — While a fragile appearance is unquestionably a great part of its charm, a headpiece should be built to withstand hours of dancing, hugging friends and relatives, and being fondled and tugged at by small children and well meaning aunts. It should be as photogenic while the band plays "Good Night, Irene" as it was when the bride made her first appearance at the back of the church.

For a list of suppliers of all kinds of millinery supplies, consult the RESOURCES DIRECTORY near the back of "I DO" VEILS

THE BASICS

Well-made bridal headpieces are constructed using a combination of three substantial fastening materials: wire, glue, and thread.

WIRE

MILLINERY WIRE

Millinery wire is a pliable steel wire wrapped in silk threads or paper. The wrapping prevents the black smudges that would otherwise occur when your hands and your work come into contact with the steel wire. It also helps prevent rust by absorbing

moisture from the air and your hands before it reaches the wire.

The most common and useful gauge of millinery wire is #19 or #20 — if there is no choice given that is undoubtedly what you are purchasing. Use this weight for structural support, and for edging a buckram frame. A higher numbered gauge indicates a lighter, thinner wire. Use it where the project requires light reinforcement — support for a leaf, a feather, or a flower petal.

Millinery wire comes in a coil, and it retains that tight spiral shape even after it is cut. That's fine only if you

are going to form it into a small circle anyway — to make a wreath or a tiara, for example. Before you can use it for any other purpose, includ-

ing a larger circle like the outer edge of a hat brim, the wire must be straightened. Bend it gently with your thumbs in the opposite direction of the curl, an inch at a time, until it is straight or very nearly so. Beginning with a straight piece of wire insures

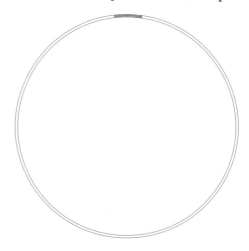

that you will be able to control its final curve; otherwise, it will buckle and twist as you try to force it around corners or unfamiliar curves.

WIRE JOINERS

To form a wire circle, use one of these soft metal tubes. Feed the ends of a piece of millinery wire into the ends of the wire joiner, then crimp the joiner over the wire with a needle-nose pliers.

If you don't have any wire joiners, overlap the ends of the wire and use a short piece of jewelry wire (or a higher gauge millinery wire) to tie them together.

JEWELRY WIRE

Use 24-gauge jewelry wire to make a beaded tiara, or a lighter gauge to hold components together temporarily as you make a prototype. Use gold-colored wire — it won't get your hands dirty or blacken over time.

Tools

NEEDLE NOSE PLIERS

These are useful for bending and crimping wire and handling tiny components like pearls and beads.

With practice, you will learn to use

them as a "third hand", meaning that you can hold something in place with

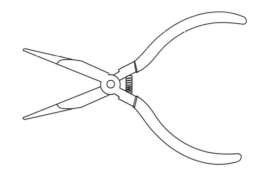

the pliers and still have enough fingers free to perform a second task with the same hand. Splurge on the kind with a spring mechanism that forces them open when your grip is released, which eliminates the wasted motion of having to manually open them every time you want to use them. Buy the smallest pair you can pick up and handle comfortably; they will quickly begin to feel like an extension of your hand.

WIRE CUTTERS

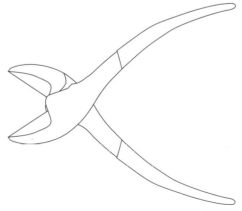

There is probably a wire cutter at the base of the jaws of your needlenose pliers, but if you're going to be making more than one headpiece, purchase a good pair of 6"-8" wire cutters — They will be stronger, to cut millinery wire effortlessly, and sharper, to completely cut through the silk or paper wrapping on the first try.

Glue

HOT GLUE

Hot glue is an effective adhesive only as long as it is truly hot, so use a hot glue gun that melts 1/2" diameter glue sticks at a relatively high temperature. Low temperature "mini" hot glue guns available at craft supply stores simply do not get the glue hot enough to allow you any working time before the glue cools and hardens.

 A glue gun icon appears in the illustrations whenever hot glue is recommend.

Use only clear hot glue sticks in a glue gun that has never been used to melt white hot glue; white residue can appear at the most inopportune places and ruin a nearly finished headpiece.

WHITE GLUE

ALLENE'S JEWEL-IT and SOBO are two fine medium-thick brands of white flexible glue. They are both easy to apply with the pointed tip of the bottle. TACKY GLUE is much thicker, and is perfect for scattering individual pearls because it holds the weight of the pearl firmly in place while it dries.

Other brands may work just as well, but read the label to be sure the glue is flexible when dry (ELMER'S glue is brittle when dry, so it is not a good substitute). Flexibility is essential to keep pearls and other components from peeling away at the slightest touch.

 Throughout the text, a glue bottle icon is used to indicate instances where white flexible glue should be used.

𝒮EWING SUPPLIES

For the parts of your headpiece that require sewing, you will need a few basic sewing supplies — a good pair of scissors, a needlenose tracing wheel, a seam ripper, an iron, etc. From time to time, these items are represented in the illustrations by icons.

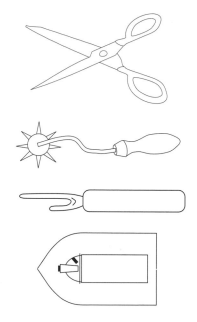

NEEDLES

The milliner's needle is the longest, thinnest, and most flexible of all hand sewing needles. At times it will behave much like a curved upholstery needle, enabling you to negotiate the impossible hairpin turns one encounters in the construction of all types of millinery. With a long flexible needle you will become a veritable speed demon as you master the craft of gathering a veil.

Milliners' needles are available in gauges from "0" to "14". The higher the gauge, the longer and thinner the needle; a size "7" is a good serviceable weight.

THREAD

Milliners, tailors, and costumers have long used silk hand sewing thread in their workrooms because it is so strong and convenient to use.

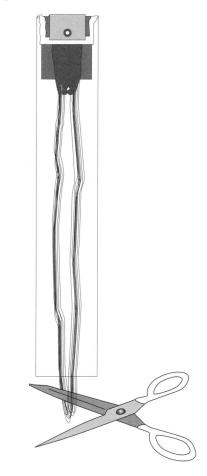

The thread is put up in 18" skeins rather than being wound onto spools. The top of the skein is secured loosely in place by the plastic packaging. Simply tear off the bottom of the package, cut through the entire skein of thread, and pull out one perfect 36" length of thread after another. The thread is pre-waxed to prevent tangling and knotting. Because it is silk, the white color blends equally well with ivory. It is quite a bit more expensive than spooled cotton/poly thread, but one skein will last one sewer more than a year and will contribute immeasurably to the speed and quality of your work.

𝒮EWING WITH ONE, TWO, OR FOUR THREADS

To save time and enhance the quality of your finished head-piece, learn the advantages of sewing with one, two, or even four threads at one time.

Sewing with one thread (or, a single thread)) means to take one length of thread, pass it through the eye of the needle, and knot one end.

Use a single thread where you'd prefer your stitches to be nearly invisible, and where there will be no stress on the stitches. Most of the steps in covering a buckram headpiece frame are best accomplished using a single thread.

Sewing with two threads (or, sewing with a double thread) means to take one length of thread, pass it through the eye of the needle, and knot both ends together. Use two threads to

gather a veil, and where medium strength is required.

Sewing with four threads means to take two lengths of thread, pass them both through the eye of the needle, and knot all four ends together. One stitch made

with four threads replaces four single-thread stitches, a real time-saver for places where the stitches will be completely hidden and where extra stitch strength is needed.

MONOFILAMENT

Monofilament is a clear thread made from a single continuous nylon fiber. The most economical way to purchase monofilament is in the form of ordinary fishing line, available in varying thicknesses described by the weight of the fish one would hope to catch with it. A 20 lb. test line has

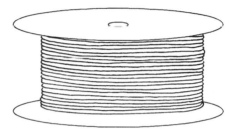

enough body to maintain the softly undulating shape of the ruffled edge without overpowering the illusion. For a softer effect — on a ruffled pouf, for example — experiment with a lower test weight.

To store a spool of monofilament without tangling, wrap it with a rubber band.

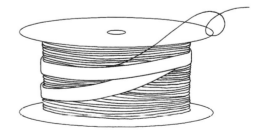

EADPIECE FRAMES

BUCKRAM FRAMES

For some headpiece shapes and most hats, you will be working with a purchased buckram frame, which provides a solid foundation for your fabrics and trimmings.

For more information on working with buckram frames, consult the HATS unit on page 86.

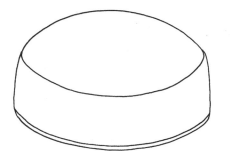

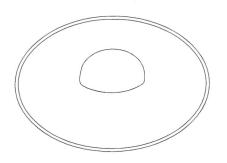

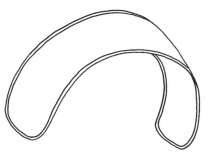

WIRE FRAMES

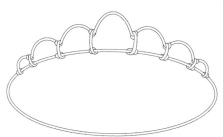

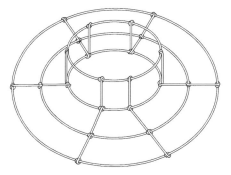

Unlike a solidly opaque buckram frame, a wire frame allows areas of transparency or translucence through and around your decoration.

Nearly any headpiece shape can be fashioned from wire rather than buckram—-a close-fitting Juliet cap, a tiara that fans out or stands up from your head, even a large picture hat. A selection of ready made wire frames are available from millinery supply sources.

For detailed instructions on working with wire frames, see JULIET CAPS (page 70) and THE LACE TIARA (page 64).

COMBS, ETC.

COMBS

Most hats and headpieces are fastened to your hair by a 3" plastic comb, available in a choice of clear plastic to blend in with the headpiece or a mottled brown tortoiseshell (also plastic) that blends with most hair colors.

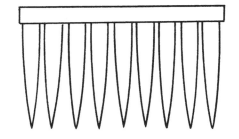

Use the entire 3" width if the headpiece will hide it well enough, or cut it to size with wire cutters. Sew the comb to the underside of your hat or headpiece, taking one stitch between each tooth. Be sure to position it so that it is invisible when your head-piece is in place.

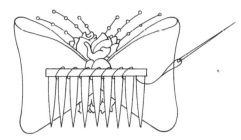

ELASTIC BRIDAL LOOPS

A comb may also be held to a head-piece with elastic bridal loop tape, normally used to fasten the buttons at the back of a gown. Glue or sew the loops to the underside of the hat or headpiece, and slide the comb's teeth — or a few bobby pins — through the loops.

HORSEHAIR BRAID

Horsehair braid is made of heavy nylon filaments resembling fishing line that have been braided together

to form a stiff yet flexible and trans-parent material.

HORSEHAIR LOOPS

If your headpiece is large or heavy, use horsehair braid to make loops that can be sewn or glued to your headpiece and bobby-pinned to your hair as a supplement to the comb.

For each loop, cut a length of 1/2" horsehair braid 2" long. Fold the horsehair in half and gather the ends together as tightly as possible. Before cutting the thread, wind it around the gathered area several times and knot it again.

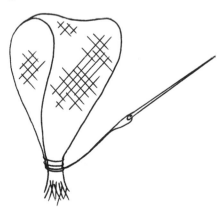

Hot glue over the gathers and the raw edges to prevent raveling and scratching your head. Sew

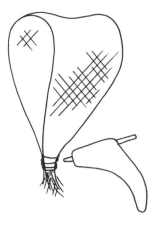

the loops to the underside of the hat or headpiece as needed.

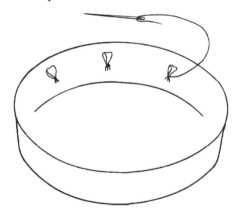

TAPES

FLORAL TAPE

Elements of a flower spray are held in place by wrapping with floral tape, a gummed self-sealing tape whose adhesive powers are released by stretching.

Begin wrapping about an inch from the end of the tape, concealing the end as you wrap the tape around the stems. Loop the floral tape around your joinings to anchor the components securely.

FOAM TAPE

Apply a self-stick foam carpet tape to the inside of a hat, headpiece, or barrette to keep it from sliding around on your head. The foam grips your hair, keeping your headpiece firmly in place.

HOOK-AND-LOOP TAPE

Use VELCRO — a popular brand name for hook-and-loop tape — to hold your detachable veil in place on your finished headpiece. To reduce the risk of having your hair becoming entangled in its grip, cut the tape into 1/4" strips — that is

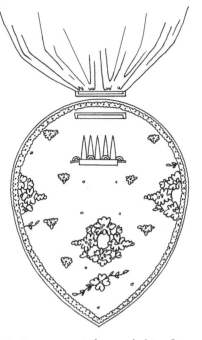

plenty to support the weight of your veil — and always position the rough hooks facing outward, so it is facing away from your hair.

You can sew hook and loop tape directly to the back of your headpiece or to the outside of a comb, just under the top ridge, before attaching the comb to your headpiece.

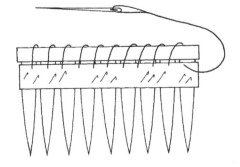

Headpiece-proof Your Work Area

Whether your work space is a dedicated sewing room or your kitchen table after the dinner dishes have been cleared, the making of bridal headpieces — with its close work on small bits of all-white materials — makes adequate lighting and a clean work environment absolutely essential.

MAKE IT EASY ON YOUR EYES: A BASIC BLACK WORK SURFACE

Working with transparent bridal illusion and a white on white color scheme can be an eyeball warping experience.

Even under perfect lighting conditions, it can be difficult to discern just where the work table ends and your veil begins! That problem can be eliminated simply by changing the color of your work surface.

The white illusion shows up very clearly when contrasted against a black background. A black work surface also eliminates fatiguing glare — Light directed onto your work is concentrated there, and any spill light is absorbed by the black rather than being bounced back up into your eyes.

If you wish, you can make the black surface a permanent change to your work table — Paint the table top with flat latex paint, or tape a heavy mat board around all the edges. For a temporary black surface, lay down a sheet of black paper or mat board, available from an art supply store.

CLEANER THAN CLEAN

To avoid soiling the white fabrics and other materials, always start with a squeaky clean workspace and keep it free of dust and fabric scraps. If possible, avoid working with dark colored fabrics and especially synthetic

furs in the same area. Nylon illusion builds up static electricity, acting as a magnet for bits of thread and lint that are tedious to remove.

Even in a spotless workroom, the natural oils in our skin attract dust particles from the air and can stain delicate white and ivory fabrics, including silk flowers. Wash your hands often, at least once an hour. Although such repeated washing may cause dryness, wait until you have finished working before applying any hand lotion, as it too may stain the fabrics.

A STITCH IN TIME...

In the interest of safety, always immediately retrieve any scraps of illusion that may fall to the floor. They are invisible and more slippery than you could possibly believe— even a tiny fragment of illusion can cause a dangerous fall.

Runaway pearls and beads should also be picked up instantly, while you still remember where they hit the floor. Otherwise, they assume their secret identity as slick ball bearings, just lying in wait to send you sliding across the room.

PUT OUT THE CAT!

Cats LOVE bridal illusion. They love to bat it around, chase it, roll in it, climb it, shed into it, and claw it to ribbons.

Shed cat hair can be removed by vacuuming the illusion with a soft brush attachment or with a sticky-tape lint remover, both of which cause incredible static. (Rips and tears can be remedied by removing the veiling and starting over!)

MIRROR, MIRROR, ON THE WALL...

Hang a large mirror right next to your work area, or prop one up on a nearby table or bookshelf. Try your headpiece on often and check your progress in the mirror. Use a hand mirror to view the sides and back of the headpiece. The reversed view of a mirror image will actually assist you in the design process — It's almost like looking at a framed picture of someone else's work, so you can critique it more honestly.

$\mathcal{E}$MBELLISHMENTS

Now that your main challenge has been met — you've chosen a basic shape for your headpiece — it's time to relax and have some real fun, selecting your trimmings.

As you select each component for your headpiece, be sure that it contributes its own distinct qualities of color, form, weight, and size. A clever designers' trick is to squint at the group of elements you're considering using in combination. If any two are indistinguishable in that blurred view, eliminate or replace one. If you choose to replace it, substitute something with more contrast, or simply repeat an existing element.

For example, ethereal baby's breath is traditionally paired with more substantial roses because of the striking contrast. Long and narrow pearl sprays enhance a bouquet of round roses and buds, while they would be lost in an arrangement of lilies of the valleys. A translucent horsehair bow makes a lovely background for compact satin hand-rolled roses, but would disappear against a cluster of equally translucent organza flowers.

Trimmings

CHOOSING YOUR TRIMMINGS

There are so many ready-to-use trimmings on the market today that you might find it difficult to narrow down the field to just a few. Luckily, most of these trimmings are astoundingly inexpensive, so give yourself permission to purchase a greater variety than you think you'll use — Having plenty of possibilities on hand is a terrific way to stimulate your creativity!

Consult the RESOURCES DIRECTORY near the back of "I DO" VEILS — There you will find a list of suppliers of all kinds of trimmings and millinery supplies.

Besides the usual craft supply stores and millinery suppliers, you can look for components and supplies at wholesale and retail florists, fabric stores, discount stores, upholstery workrooms, and candy and cake decorating suppliers. They are occasionally all good supplementary sources.

Keep an eye out at garage and estate sales, vintage clothing stores, resale shops, and antique fairs for unusual decorative items — flowers, feathers,and other trimmings—-that might first have to be liberated from whatever they're dubiously decorating at the moment.

Of course you can create some of your own components from a few basic supplies like individual pearls and silk flowers. But do search carefully through all of the supply resources first to be sure you're not spending hours duplicating something that could be purchased for only a few pennies.

Here, then, are the building blocks for your own designs — the stepping stones to your own exciting headpiece creations!

PEARLS

Sized by the millimeter, faux pearls can be tiny and ultra-feminine or huge and theatrical.

Apply them one at a time — with thread or glue — or by the strand, in drops, or strung on monofilament or wire.

To de-emphasize the holes in the pearls, glue or sew them in place so that the holes are oriented from side to side. Rather than trying to pick up and manipulate such tiny objects with the fingers — which might eventually mean covering your hands in white glue or burning them with the hot glue gun — use a straight pin to pick up one at a time, apply glue to it, and place it into position.

PEARL SPRAYS

Pearl sprays are made from individual pearls glued at intervals to a grouping of monofilament strands.

The monofilament is nearly invisible, giving the effect of pearls dancing a perfectly choreographed ballet over and around your headpiece.

Looped pearl sprays are formed by including both ends of the monofilament in the stem wrapping.

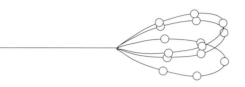

More substantial pearl sprays are formed on heavy wire stems wrapped in floral tape, rather than monofilament. These white opaque stems can be bent into position on the finished headpiece, and are used for making crowns.

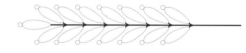

$\mathcal{P}$EARL LEAVES AND FLOWERS

Stylized flowers and leaves — formed from individual pearls threaded onto bent and twisted wires — are interesting and flexible components for headpiece design. Use them for textural variety with silk flowers, or alone for a contemporary design.

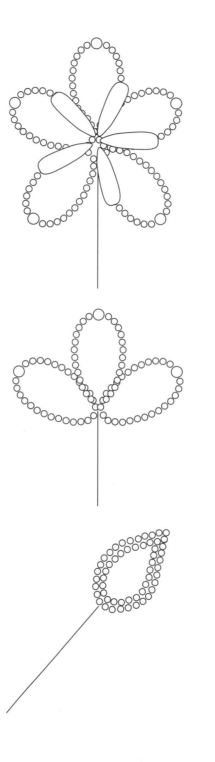

$\mathcal{P}$EARL PEPS

At the center of any living flower is a group of pistils and stamens (look it up!). They look like little flexible wires with pearls at the top — Which, coincidentally, is also a pretty good description of pearl peps. Use stems of pearl peps to add a touch of realism to your handmade flowers.

$\mathcal{P}$EARL DROPS

Dangle tear-drop or oval pearls from a headpiece by sewing with a double thread through the pearl drop, through a tiny bead or pearl, and back through the pearl drop to the headpiece.

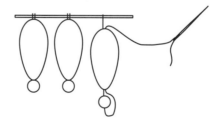

Some drops have a wire loop threaded through their centers for easy sewing — Crimp the loop with your needle nose pliers to prevent the thread from slipping out.

PEARL STRANDS

Round or flat-back pearls glued at tight intervals to a string or wire arc used where a quick application of closely and evenly spaced pearls is important, such as the edging on a veil.

Use pearls with wire strands only where the pearls must stand on their own and hold their own shape.

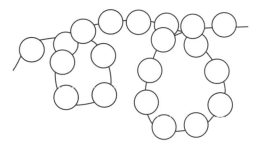

PEARL HEADBANDS AND BRAIDS

These are usually sold as long straight lengths, with millinery wire at either end that must be joined to form a circle for a halo or V-band. You can also use them to make large dramatic loops or figure 8's.

BEADED MOTIFS

A design in pearls, beads, and sequins sewn to a backing of organza and reinforced with glue can be used as a focal point for a V-band or a sophisticated hat. Form a pattern of smaller motifs on a headpiece, or scatter tiny ones on a veil or pouf.

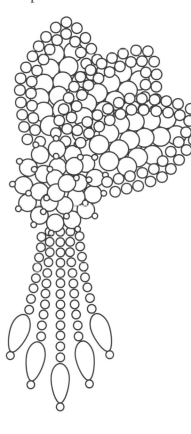

RHINESTONES

Foil-backed rhinestones are rarely used in bridal millinery. Although

they sparkle like diamonds from a distance, in photographs they can emerge as unsightly black dots. The silver foil backing also tends to darken over time, giving the stones a greyish cast. Strands of tiny crystal rhinestones preset into white plastic settings hold

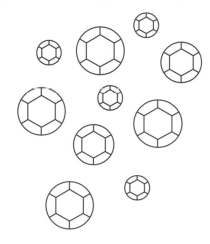

up much better, and their diminutive size should not pose a risk to the wedding photographs.

SEQUINS

Clear or iridescent sequins, on the other hand, impart an equally brilliant sparkle that seems to come from nowhere as the sequins all but disappear into the shadows of the fabric, lace, or other trimmings. They can be easily applied with white glue. Sequins are sized by the millimeter — Five-millimeter faceted sequins are the most commonly used.

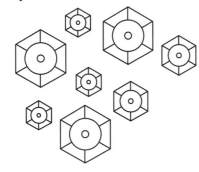

AUSTRIAN CRYSTAL BEADS

Austrian crystal beads and drops are more expensive than sequins, but they have an opulent sparkle that rivals the forbidden rhinestone, and they have no foil backing to make them show up as black dots in a photograph. Instead, light is reflected by their carefully cut facets and three-dimensional lead crystal form. Beads called

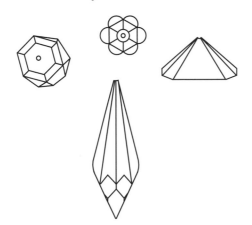

simply "crystals" are perfectly clear, while "aurora borealis crystals" have a fired-on iridescent finish. They are sized by the millimeter, have holes for sewing or stringing on wire, and are available in a variety of shapes, including tiny flowers.

BEAD SPRAYS

Glued at intervals on strands of monofilament, bead sprays are made in the same way as pearl sprays, with plastic, glass, or Austrian crystal beads substituted for the pearls. Plastic and glass beads are not as expensive as the crystals, but they also do not possess the same glitter. Avoid glass beads lined with silver, as they may blacken over time.

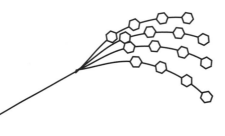

SILK FLOWERS

Every imaginable flower has been recreated in fabric, from the daintiest spring apple blossom to the most dramatic of tropical orchids.

White and ivory bridal flowers almost always have matching stems and

leaves. Natural green stems and leaves disrupt the pale monochromatic color scheme, and sometimes photograph as black voids in a headpiece design. Of course there are exceptions — For a country garden look, a subtle green is sometimes combined with ivory, but it is almost never used with white.

FLOWER SPRAYS

A spray is a grouping of individual flowers, buds, and leaves, twisted together on the same main stem. It may be a bouquet of several of the same flower, a stem combining one or more fully blossomed flowers with

leaves and buds of the same variety, or a more complex

design harmonizing several different flowers with pearl sprays or other components.

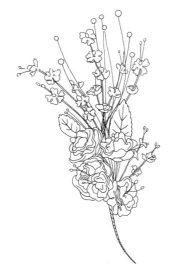

A graduated floral spray is a horizontal arrangement, with a large flower at the center and increasingly smaller

ones at either side. Wreath sprays range from 10" to 20" in length, and

are meant to encircle the head. They may or may not be graduated.

You can separate a purchased spray to use the flowers in another arrangement. Try grasping the main stem and firmly tugging an individual flower out. If tugging does not release the flowers, unwind the floral tape from the bottom until the flowers fall free.

If you are using individual flowers in your headpiece design, form them into small sprays first for greater sta-

bility and ease of handling. Or, customize your floral sprays by introducing new flowers into them — Wind the wire stems of individual flowers or other components around the thickest part of the spray's stem, and wrap the stem with floral tape.

Falls

Usc a fall — a cascading floral spray including pearl sprays and other components — at the side of a V-band or halo for an asymmetrical look, or sew it to a comb or barrette for a simple side or back decoration.

HANDMADE FLOWERS

For a couture designer touch, make stylized flowers from scraps of the fabric in your gown. For directions on making many different kinds of fabric and ribbon flowers, turn to page 25.

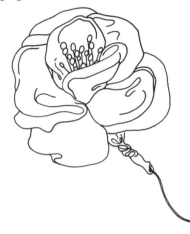

RIBBON

Satin ribbon is really nothing more than a very, very narrow satin fabric. It is available in widths as tiny as

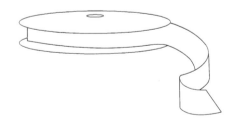

1/16 of an inch. Single-face satin has a shiny satin surface on the right side and a matte taffeta surface on the reverse, while double-face satin is heavier in weight and feel and has a satin surface on both sides.

Some polyester satin ribbons are permanently "warped" — that is, the selvage is woven so tightly that the ribbon has a wavy appearance that cannot be flattened by pressing. Nylon satin ribbon can be pressed flat even if it is "warped", and it can also be easily dyed. Silk satin ribbon has a rich, subtle luster rather than a real shine, and is more expensive than either polyester or nylon.

LOVE KNOTS

An old tradition states that ribbon streamers on a bridal veil must

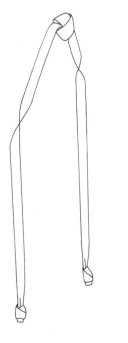

have their ends knotted to keep the bride's good luck from running out the bottom. A charming addition to some headpiece styles is a grouping of 1/16" or 1/8" ribbons, of the same general length but varied somewhat, all knotted at the bottom. Cut 3 to 5 equal lengths, twice the average finished length. If possible, simply tie them around the headpiece frame at the desired location. Or, knot each one close to but not exactly at the center, and sew or glue the center knots to the headpiece.

Don't forget to knot the ends!

BOWS

From the romantically frilly to the most elegantly tailored, bows are a beautiful way to incorporate fabric from your gown into your headpiece. A bow makes a soft foundation for

your headpiece, or a simple headpiece all on its own for your bridesmaids or flower girls. Turn to page 30 for directions on making bows from a variety of materials.

Lace

Some types of lace can be cut apart so that you can use the individual lace motifs in your headpiece design — Re-embroidered Alencon lace (pronounced: Uh-LAHN-sahn) has a wonderful three-dimensional quality, and is available plain or embellished with beads, sequins, or pearls. Featuring

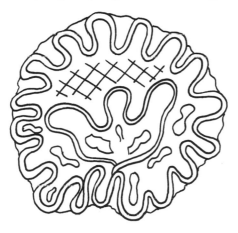

individually formed motifs, Venice lace (pronounced: veh-NEESE) is easily recognized because it is the only type of lace not backed with netting.

When cutting apart the lace motifs, be sure to cut around the entire motif, not through it, to prevent raveling. The cord that outlines the Alencon motifs is a continuous one, so you will be forced to cut through it occasionally — Dab a bit of flexible white glue onto those areas as an added precaution against raveling.

Horsehair Braid

Horsehair braid is made of heavy nylon filaments resembling fishing line that have been braided together

to form a stiff yet flexible and transparent material. It is available in different weights in widths ranging from 1/2" to 12", and comes in a wide variety of colors. Use it for bows, either by itself or to lend support to a ribbon or fabric bow, and for making bobby pin loops to help secure your headpiece to your head (see MATERIALS AND SUPPLIES, page 13)

Because it is woven on the bias, horsehair can be manipulated into some wild contemporary configurations, such as the decoration at the side of this cloche hat. Horsehair braid is also available accordion pleated, which gives it a very different kind of dimension and design quality. A wider horsehair braid can even be used to make a brim for a pillbox or other small hat.

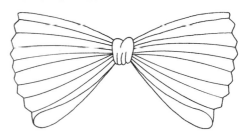

Horsehair Tubing

1/4" tubular horsehair can be used to make a stylized flower or bow, or as a covering for millinery wire where the wire would otherwise remain exposed. Prevent the ends from raveling with an application of glue.

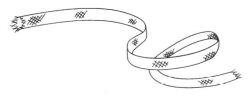

ℛouleau
(PRONOUNCED: ROO-LOW)

Wired rouleau is a purchased trim with a chic contemporary look. It consists of a narrow turned tube of bias-cut satin fabric ("rouleau" is French for "tube"), padded with string or yarn. It has a pliable wire running through it, which allows it to be easily shaped. Use wired rouleau or horsehair tubing to make stylized bows, loops, or flowers.

𝒟yes

You can dye fabrics and trimmings made of cotton, linen, wool, silk, rayon, or nylon with RIT or TINTEX dyes, available in drug, hardware, grocery, and craft stores. Always test for

color and intensity on a scrap first. For some shades of beige and ivory, dyeing in a solution of tea or coffee may give you a better color than a commercial dye.

Most lace will accept the dye differently where the pattern is dense than it does in the more sparsely decorated areas, resulting in a variegation that is part of its charm.

Most flowers called silk are actually rayon, so they can be dyed easily to any color. Because the flowers are constructed with water soluble glues, they should be immersed in the dye for only a few seconds, so test the color strength of the dye solution by experimenting with a stray bud or leaf. Rinse the flowers under cold running water to remove the excess dye, and gently shake or pat out the excess water.

Allow the flowers to air dry — right side up — overnight on paper towels.

For a large quantity or a specific color match, arrange to have the flowers dyed by your supplier.

Pearls accept dyes easily and quickly. Tie the pearls loosely in a pouch made from a scrap of bridal illusion and dip the entire package into the dye solution.

That way, all the pearls will be removed from the dye at the same time, insuring even color and no escapees.

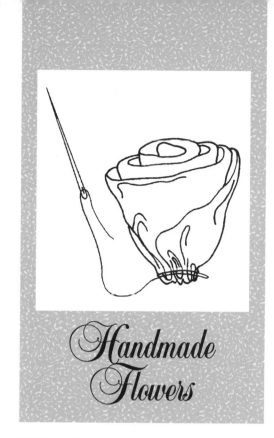

Handmade Flowers

While silk flowers tend to be quite realistic, most handmade flowers have a more stylized appearance — They are meant to capture the spirit of a flower rather than its exact form.

Because of their stylized look, handmade flowers are frequently used for contemporary or high-style couture headpieces. Coincidentally, they are just as at home in a Victorian or other traditional setting, where their charm lies in looking handmade.

Handmade flowers of fabric or ribbon are a personalized custom detail that helps to distinguish a gown and headpiece as a true ensemble.

Hand-Rolled Fabric Roses

Roses are easiest to make in light or medium weight fabrics like silk shantung, organza, or satin.

Instructions are given for a 2" rose. For a different size, vary the length and width of your bias strip.

For each flower, cut a bias strip of fabric 18" long and 3" wide. Fold the fabric strip lengthwise with the right sides together, and round the corners.

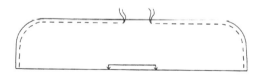

Using a 1/4" seam allowance, sew the fabric into a tube, leaving a 2" opening at the center of the long edge.

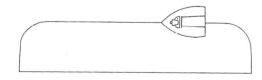

Turn the tube right side out through the opening and press the seam flat, turning in the remaining raw edges. Do NOT press the folded edge.

Gather along the entire sewn edge — Take stitches that are 1/4" apart, through just a few threads of your fabric.

Pull the thread until the gathering measures 8". Knot the thread but don't bother to cut it, and distribute the fullness evenly.

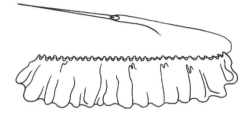

Use the threaded end of your fabric as the center of your rose. Wind the rest of the gathered edge — just an inch or two at a time — tightly around the center, then secure it with stitches that go all the way through the previously wound layers.

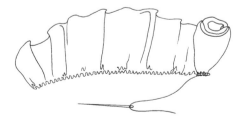

When the entire rose has been wound and stitched, take three or four more stitches through the entire base for extra security. Knot the thread and cut it.

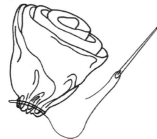

A hand-rolled rose can be crafted from a straight length of ribbon instead of a bias fabric tube, but it will not have the same lush character as the fabric rose because of the ribbon's straight grain and single layer construction.

HAND-ROLLED ROSEBUDS

For each bud, cut a bias strip 4-1/2" long and 3" wide. Aside from gathering the tube to a length of just 2-1/2" rather than 8", use the same techniques as for the rose. Due to the shorter length of the bias tube, the bud will remain tightly closed rather than fanning out in the shape of a rose.

AN ELEGANT PETALED ROSE

To make a 3" flower, cut four 5" squares of fabric, and fold them into triangles. Lap the folded edges of the triangles over each other as if you were closing a cardboard box.

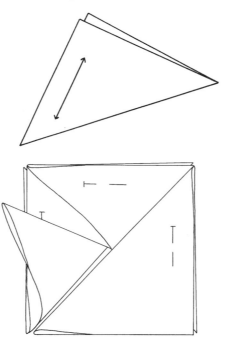

Gather around the entire outside edge of the square as tightly as possible, causing the petals to open and cup around the center of the flower.

To camouflage the gathering, add a decorative button at the center of the flower.

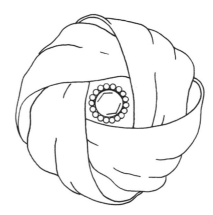

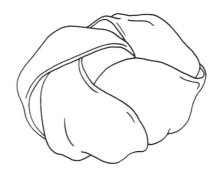

A QUICK AND EASY ROSETTE

For a 2-1/2" flower, cut a length of ribbon 2" wide and 12" long. Mark 5 even triangles — each 4" apart — on the wrong side of the ribbon, and cut away the diagonals at both ends. Using a double thread and a running stitch, gather the entire length of the zigzag line as tightly as

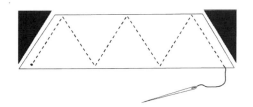

possible. Arrange the petals and sew the flower into a circle.

ℐNDIVIDUAL PETALS

These single petals are useful for creating different types of flat stylized flowers. The petals can also be used individually or added to a flower spray.

CIRCULAR PETALS

Cut a circle of fabric for each petal. Fold the circle in half, on the bias. Gather the raw edges as tightly as

possible, and wrap the thread around the gathers several times before knotting and cutting your thread.

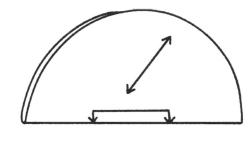

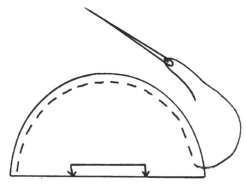

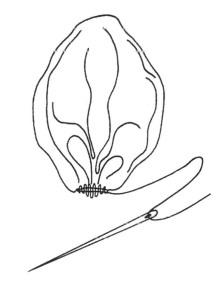

FAIRY PETALS

Form a petal shape from the center of a length of wire, twisting the ends of the wire into a stem.

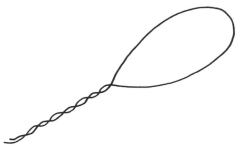

Cut a circle of tulle or chiffon and stretch it gently over the form.

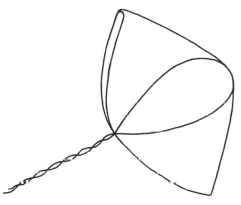

Sew or wire the fabric at the base of the petal.

RIBBON PETALS

To make a simple flower petal, cut a length of ribbon two to four times its width, and clip a triangle out of the two bottom corners.

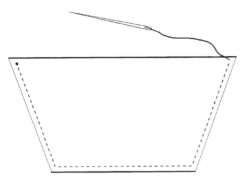

Using a running stitch, gather the ends and the short edge of the ribbon as tightly as possible.

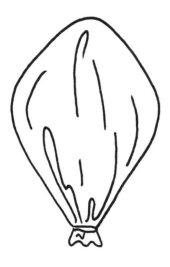

LACE PETALS

Cut motifs from Alencon or Venice lace trim or fabric. For each lace petal, form a shaped support from the center of a length of wire, twisting the ends of the wire into a stem. Glue the wire to the back of each petal. Once the glue has dried, your petals can be bent and shaped.

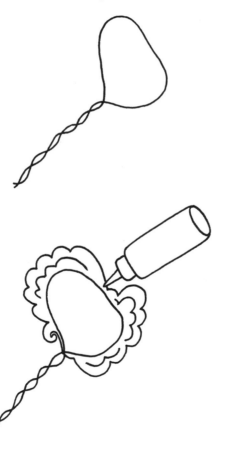

FORMING THE FLOWERS

Use your petals to make a number of different flowers.

APPLE BLOSSOMS

Group 3-6 petals around a center for a simple blossom. For a more complex design, combine two or more layers of petals in different sizes. Place the petals side by side or overlap them slightly.

ROSES

To form a three-dimensional rose, group the petals around a stem of pearl peps, overlapping them and graduating the size of the petals toward the outside of the rose. Wrap the stem in floral tape.

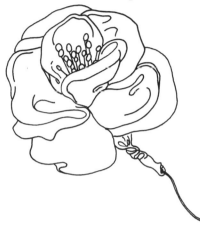

BUDS

To form a bud from a circular petal or ribbon petal, pull the two ends of the gathering to the front and sew them tightly together. For added dimension, enfold a smaller petal inside of a larger one.

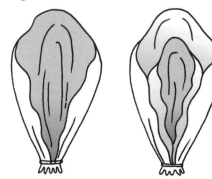

*D*ESIGN DETAILS

Let your handmade flowers and buds speak for themselves, or dress them up a bit by adding one of these couture touches —

A PEARL PEP CENTER

Push a stem of pearl peps or a pearl spray through the center of your

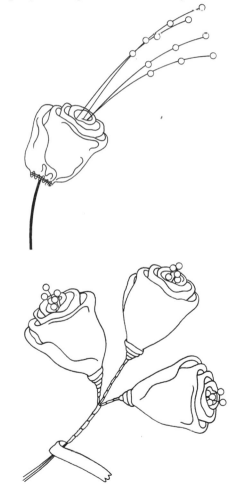

flower. Hot glue the stem underneath and cut off the excess if the flower is being applied directly to the headpiece. Or, twist several stems together with floral tape to make a spray of flowers.

COMBINE MATERIALS

For variety, combine different materials within the same flower. For example, include petals of organza ribbon or lightweight lace in a taffeta flower.

ADD COLOR

To add a hint of color, cut a tiny hole in a 3/4" square of pastel chiffon and slide it onto the pearl pep stem before inserting it into the center of the flower or bud. Use a color that echoes the shade of the bridesmaids' dresses, or add a touch of pink or peach to accent the blush in your cheeks.

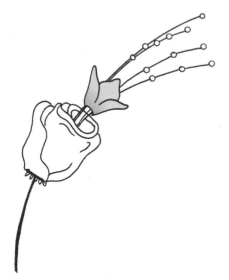

ADD A DESIGNER CENTER

A glamorous button or a grouping of individual pearls makes an attractive center for a two-dimensional flower. Or, cover the center with a tiny rosette.

Bows

Hand-sculpted bows made from ribbon or a fabric to match your gown add a real couture touch to your headpiece. A bow makes a lovely foundation for a headpiece, providing a background to showcase an arrangement of flowers, pearls, and other components.

Rarely fabricated from just a single length of ribbon, your bow's shape is carefully controlled by assembling individual loops of ribbon or bias-cut strips of fabric. A diverse variety of other materials lend themselves to bow making, from wired rouleau to horsehair braid.

RIBBON BOWS

If the memory of the lopsided ribbons tied at the ends of your braids when you were a child has clouded your feeling toward bows, it's time to put that image to rest. You can easily make a perfect ribbon bow — One that any grownup would be proud to wear!

MATERIALS

Ribbon

1/2" horsehair braid (optional)

Trimmings of your choice

A BASIC RIBBON BOW

Cut a length of ribbon that measures twice the length of your finished bow plus 2" — For example, a 6" bow requires 14" of ribbon. Fold the length in half and mark the center lightly with a pencil.

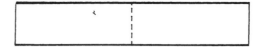

Place the two free ends over the center mark, overlapping them 1". Without flattening the loops, grasp the center of the bow and verify the finished measurement. Adjust the overlap if necessary, and cut off any excess — the total overlap should not exceed 1" or the width of the ribbon.

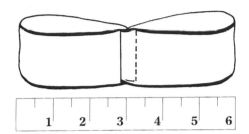

Gather the center of the bow tightly by hand through all layers. Before cutting the thread, wrap it firmly around the gathered center several times and knot it a second time for extra stability.

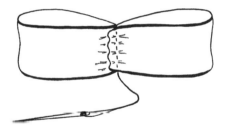

THE CENTER KNOT

Cut a length of ribbon 3"-4" long. Pleat the ribbon at one end, and tack it to the back of the center of the gathered bow.

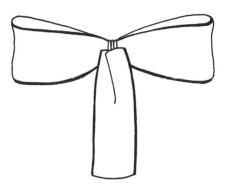

Wrap the ribbon around the bow — adjusting the tension to fit your design — and pleat the remaining end in the opposite direction from the

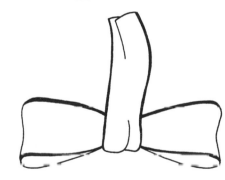

first. For a clean finish, turn under a seam allowance that will just cover the raw edges on the first end, and clip away any excess.

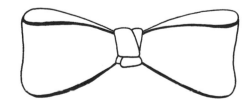

For a very wide bow, use a narrower ribbon for the center wrapping, or

fold back one or both edges of the wider ribbon to narrow it.

STREAMERS

Streamers are the leftover ends of the ribbon that would extend down from the bow if it were actually hand tied.

Fashion both streamers from one piece of ribbon — Cut a length of ribbon a little longer than twice the finished measurement of the streamers, and fold the center of the ribbon into a box pleat. Fold the center at the

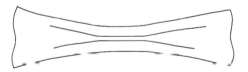

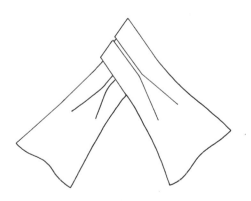

desired angle, and sew your streamers to the back of the center knot.

Cut the ends of the streamers at an angle or a chevron — Do not cut them straight across because the ribbon will ravel. Cut one streamer slightly longer than the other for a more natural look.

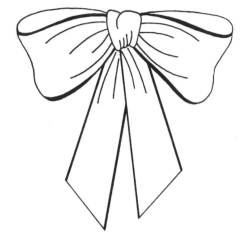

REINFORCE WITH HORSEHAIR

To give your ribbon bow greater substance, stiffen the edges with 1/2" horsehair braid.

Only the edges of a ribbon can be stiffened with horsehair, not the entire width (Horsehair is woven on the bias, so it would buckle and twist if sewn to both edges of your straight-grain ribbon). Using a medium length straight stitch, sew the horsehair as close to the ribbon's tiny selvage edge as possible. The inner edge of the horsehair remains free.

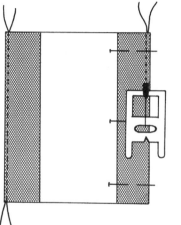

ℱ𝒶BRIC BOWS

Customize your bow by incorporating the matching lace or fabric from your gown. Order extra fabric through your bridal salon, or ask your dressmaker for scraps.

MATERIALS

Fabric

Horsehair braid (optional)

Trimmings of your choice

The simplest way to make a fabric bow is to cut a strip of fabric — on the straight grain — to the desired width. Serge the edges or cover them with a trimming, and proceed as for a ribbon bow. If your design calls for streamers, cut another strip of fabric — also on the straight grain — and clean finish the edges with a rolled hem or a serger.

𝒜 FABRIC BOW STIFFENED WITH HORSEHAIR BRAID

If you wish to support your fabric bow with horsehair braid to hold its shape, your fabric must be cut on the bias to work with the horsehair's bias weave. The finished width of your bow is dictated by the width of the horsehair.

Cut a long bias strip twice the finished width plus 1-1/4". Using a 5/8" seam allowance — and being careful not to stretch the bias — sew the strip into a tube, and press. Insert the horsehair into the tube.

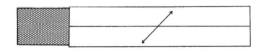

If you wish, you can eliminate the seam — Trim the long edges of the fabric with pinking shears and gently press under both edges around the horsehair so that they overlap on the inside of the bow's loops.

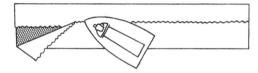

Cut the fabric and the horsehair to length, and proceed as for a ribbon bow.

STREAMERS

Make another bias tube and turn the angled ends into the tube for hand finishing. Do not include any horsehair in the streamers.

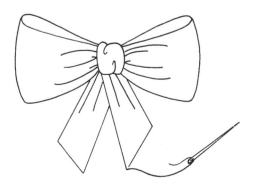

ALTERNATE MATERIALS

Be adventurous in experimenting with potential materials for your bows. Incorporating and combining unexpected elements is a major contributor to an exciting headpiece design.

FRENCH RIBBON

French ribbon is made from a narrow strip of fabric with a thin pliable wire inserted through its serged edges. It is available in a variety of widths, colors, and patterns from any good craft or fabric shop. French ribbon makes a very nice soft bow that requires no

further stiffening. The wired edges of the ribbon are meant to crinkle a bit, giving the bow an old-fashioned handmade quality.

LACE

Lace fabrics and trims make beautiful bows, and can be supported relatively

invisibly with horsehair. Or, sew or glue a lace edging or appliques to a plain ribbon bow.

To reduce bulk at the center of a bow, do not continue any applied trimmings all the way to the ends of the ribbon that will be overlapped at the center. The center wrapping will disguise the gap in the trimming.

FRENCH VEILING

French veiling is weightless and airy, and can be handled just like ribbon. To give a small bow more substance, fold the French veiling in half before proceeding, or use a double layer for a larger bow. Use ribbon or fabric for your center knot, or conceal the gathered center with flowers.

ILLUSION OR MALINE

Cut your illusion twice the finished width of your bow and turn both edges in to meet at the center. Fold it in half again to completely disguise the edges.

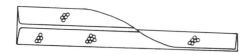

WIRED ROULEAU OR PEARLS

For a contemporary bride, wired rouleau can be formed into a multi-looped stylized bow. Wind the rouleau as many times as you like around a piece of cardboard. Slide the rouleau off the cardboard, and secure the center tightly with a short

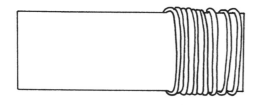

length of wire. Wrap the center with ribbon, or wind it several times with another length of rouleau. Gently pull the wired loops into position.

Use the same technique to make a bow with wired pearls.

HORSEHAIR BRAID

Rather than always relegating it to a supporting role, let horsehair take center stage for a change. It is well able to stand on its own, and can be scattered with lace appliques or edged with pearls or sequins. Just for

fun, try loops that twist in the middle, or fold the horsehair lengthwise — Remember, horsehair is woven on the bias, so it may take unexpected and wonderful shapes and hold them all on its own.

VARIATIONS ON A THEME

Vary the shape of your bow to fit the mood of your wedding — Your bow can be frilly and feminine, serene and tailored, or old-fashioned and romantic.

A TAILORED BOW

For a squarer, more tailored bow, replace the center gathering with an inverted box pleat.

MULTIPLE BOWS

You can include additional bows in the same center knot. Create visual depth by graduating their size or combining different materials.

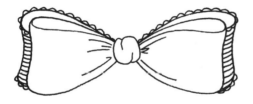

AN OLD-FASHIONED BOW

To give your bow a natural droop, tack the backs of the loops together near the base of the center knot. If

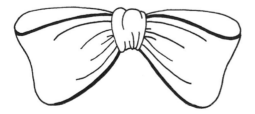

two bows are included in the same canter wrapping, tack them in oppo-

site directions for an old-fashioned "Mary Jane" bow.

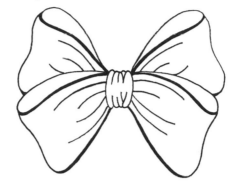

ℐNDIVIDUAL BOW LOOPS

Bow loops with wired stems are versatile components, useful for adding small bits of color or gown fabric to your headpiece.

MATERIALS

Ribbon (or ribbon made from fabric)

Jewelry wire

Floral tape

FORMING THE LOOPS

Cut a length of ribbon, and gather the ends together as tightly as possible. Wrap the center of a length of jewelry wire tightly around the gathering and twist the ends of the wire together to form a stem. Cover the stem with floral tape.

Cluster several bow loops together to make a very full bow or a stylized "flower".

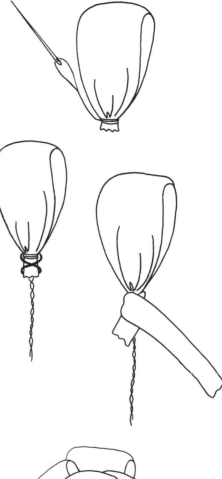

VEILS

While not every bridal hat and headpiece is finished off with a veil, it is certainly true that nothing says, "This is not your average white ball gown" more eloquently than a surrounding cloud of illusion.

Veils may be made in any length, any fullness, with any number of tiers, and adorned with scattered pearls, sequins, or lace appliques. Your veil might even be made entirely of lace, point d'esprit, or another sheer lightweight fabric. The edge can be embellished with pearls, lace, or ribbon. There may be a pouf at the back, or a blusher to be lifted from your face for your first kiss.

In other words, there are no rules and no limits beyond your own imagination.

Veil Lengths

The length of your veil is determined by the style of your wedding and the shape of your gown. In general, a longer veil looks more formal than a shorter one. While a very full ball gown can balance a number of different veil lengths, a sheath gown looks best with a shorter veil.

If you are uncertain about the right length veil for you, wait until your headpiece is completed, then try your entire wedding outfit on in front of a full-length mirror. Pin a long length of illusion to your headpiece — Or ask a friend to hold it there — so you can see the effect. If it seems too long, cut a little bit of it away at a time until you are satisfied with the total picture.

BLUSHER

A blusher is worn over your face as you walk down the aisle. The blusher is an emblem of purity, and a holdover from the days of arranged marriages, when the groom would literally see his bride's face for the first time at the moment of their marriage. The blusher may be lifted away at the altar by the person giving you away, or left in place until the officiant says the words "You may kiss the bride!" — It is then removed by your new husband as a symbol of the undressing of his new wife.

Because of its strong association with virginity, a blusher should technically never be worn for a second marriage or by an obviously pregnant bride. The length of the blusher depends upon the style of the headpiece and the wedding — It traditionally just touches the shoulders, but can be longer provided it can still be lifted away easily.

SHOULDER LENGTH

Sometimes called a Madonna or Flyaway veil, a shoulder length veil touches your shoulders or covers them slightly. The standard length is 24", although yours may range from 18" to 27".

LBOW LENGTH

Just as you might expect, an elbow length veil just reaches your elbows or your waist. It may range from 28" to 36" in length — 30" is the most common length.

INGERTIP

A fingertip veil is usually 48" long, although it may range from 36" to 50" in order to just graze your fingertips when your fingers are extended.

WALTZ LENGTH

Sometimes called a Ballerina or Walking veil, the waltz length veil should terminate 8" to 12" above the floor, placing the length between mid-calf and just above the ankles. The usual length of a waltz length veil is 54" to 60".

CHAPEL LENGTH

A chapel length veil just skims or clears the floor with no excess trailing behind. Oddly, the industry standard for this length is 90", which on most brides would certainly be too long to meet that definition (you'd have to be nearly eight feet tall!).

CATHEDRAL LENGTH

A cathedral length veil has a very long train — sometimes longer than the gown itself — following the bride down the aisle. Usually reserved for very formal weddings, the veil ranges between 3 yds. and 5 yds. (108" to 180"). At least 1 foot of the veil should trail on the floor. Some brides wear a cathedral length veil with a floor length dress to give the impression of a long train.

Veil Styles

The shape of your veil and any applied decoration should complement your gown, not compete with it. For example, while a short multi-tiered veil gives good balance to a "mermaid" style gown or a sheath dress, it probably has too many horizontal lines to be worn with a suit. Similarly, if your gown is heavily beaded, resist scattering the veil with more beads.

SINGLE TIERED VEIL

Made with just one layer of illusion, this is the most common type of veil. It is transparent enough to allow all of the detail on your gown to show through, and is not likely to steal focus from you or your gown.

##

For extra fullness, wear a veil with more than one layer of illusion — The bottom layers act as a petticoat for the top layers, billowing them out behind you.

EART-SHAPED VEIL

Three separate sections are gathered together to give the effect of a multi-tiered veil without as much fullness. Edge the sections with narrow satin ribbon for definition (otherwise, the veil may just look torn).

ANTILLA

Derived from Spanish folk dress, a mantilla was originally worn over a high decorative comb. The front of an ungathered circle or oval of lace — or illusion edged with lace — is laid over the top of the headpiece, typically a Juliet cap or other close-fitting shape. A mantilla may be any length.

CASCADE

A two tiered style whose shorter top tier may do double duty as a built-in blusher. The tiers may be of any length.

The Art of Illusion

Most bridal veils are made from a very fine nylon netting called illusion, available from fabric stores, craft supply stores, and millinery suppliers.

Illusion comes in white and ivory, in widths of 72" and 108". A pale off-white shade called "Candlelight," "Diamond White," or "Silk White," has become popular for use with white silk wedding gowns — Since silk fabric is never a true white, a stark white veil can make a silk gown appear dingy, while an ivory veil would be much too dark.

If at all possible, wait to purchase your illusion until just before you are ready to use it, and even then store it draped across the back of a chair rather than leaving it folded up inside the bag, so it does not have a chance to develop any wrinkles.

Inspect your illusion for holes and tears before it is cut from the bolt. Try not to purchase the last piece of illusion on the bolt — It usually has a lot of wrinkles and creases that may prove impossible to press out.

Unusual Materials

If you are looking for something a little bit out of the ordinary, there are a number of alternatives to plain bridal illusion. When selecting one of these materials, be sure it will not overpower the detailing on your gown or headpiece.

SILK ILLUSION

Silk illusion is much finer and softer than nylon, and a great deal more expensive. It does have a lovely ethereal quality, but it is extremely fragile. Because it is so rarely used, silk illusion may be difficult to find.

ENGLISH NET

English net is 100% cotton. It has a more substantial look and feel than nylon illusion, and is more opaque.

English net's advantage is that it will hold a true rolled edge — That is, an edge rolled inward on itself with your fingers will remain in place. (Polyester English net is not a suitable substitute for cotton — it is heavy and stiff and will not hold a rolled edge.) English net may go completely limp in the rain or in high humidity.

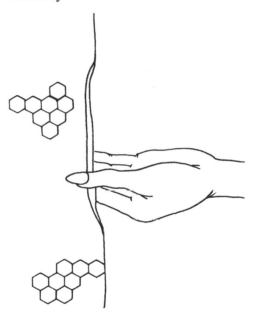

FRENCH VEILING (ALSO CALLED RUSSIAN VEILING)

A stiffer net with a large diamond-shaped pattern, French veiling is available in several widths, the most common being 9". It is available studded with pearls, rhinestones, or even chenille pompons.

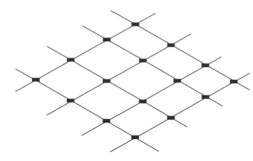

French veiling is normally used as a face veil or a decorative accent. It can be dyed easily for use on bridesmaids' headpieces..

MALINE

Maline is a much finer and softer nylon netting than bridal illusion. It is used mainly for face veils and accent decoration — and for bridesmaids' headpieces, because it is available in such a wide range of colors. Maline tears very easily.

POINT D'ESPRIT

A heavier and more opaque netting scattered with tiny dots. Most of the point d'esprit available today is made of polyester, so it is quite stiff and uncooperative, but if you search for it you might manage to put your hands on a piece of imported cotton or silk point d'esprit, which should be much lighter. Cotton or silk point d'esprit should hold a true rolled edge, the same as English net.

LACE

Choose a lightweight lace like Chantilly or Schiffli for your lace veil, and finish the veil with a lace edging.

If you want to use point d'esprit or lace for your veil, avoid any

gathering that could make the veil look bunchy — Design your headpiece as an ungathered mantilla, edged with a wide lace.

For a veil with an all over lace pattern that has its own finished edge, purchase a fine quality Belgian or Irish lace oval or round tablecloth (no kidding!). Gather a small section at one end of the tablecloth to attach it to your veil, or lay it over your headpiece like a mantilla.

CUTTING ILLUSION

For most veils, use the full width of the widest illusion available, 108". Choose 72" illusion only for a veil elbow length or shorter, to avoid a skimpy look. Occasionally you can find illusion 144" wide, which is great for a Cathedral length veil. Never piece the illusion to add additional width — the unsightly seams are impossible to disguise.

108" illusion is folded in quarters to fit a bolt that is 27" wide — To keep it manageable, do not unfold the illusion before cutting. Cut across the illusion exactly perpendicular to the edge, as any other angle will cause a zigzag effect when the illusion is unfolded.

Since illusion is transparent, it is easy

to cut a perfectly straight line with a rotary cutter or electric scissors by following a grid line on your rotary cutting mat. Or, cut it with ordinary sharp sewing shears.

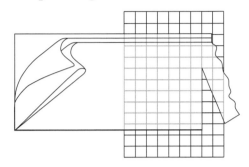

CUTTING A TWO TIERED VEIL

For a two tiered veil or a cascade veil, combine the measurements for both tiers and cut the illusion in one piece. For example, if the tiers are to measure 24" and 36", the total cut length will be 60".

After cutting the length that you need, press a crease along the line dividing the two tiers.

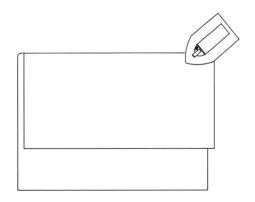

CUTTING A HEART-SHAPED VEIL

A heart-shaped veil is made in three sections. Cut one long center section, and a smaller one for either side.

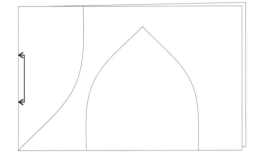

ROUNDING THE CORNERS

On an undecorated veil, the bottom corners can be rounded or left square, but they must be rounded if your veil is to be edged with pearls or ribbon, or if you will be ruffling the edge with monofilament.

If the corners of your veil are to be rounded, save time and insure perfect symmetry by cutting them together. Cut a gentle curve — around the bottom corners of the illusion only — using a 10"-12" radius. Make a paper or cardboard template if you wish.

☞ATHERING THE VEIL

If your veil will have an edging or a scattered decoration, apply those to the flat illusion before gathering it (See page 45 for edging suggestions and directions, and page 49 for help with scattered decoration).

Press out the vertical folds in the illusion before gathering your veil.

Use a double thread to gather your veil (See page 11). The gathering may be worked with either the back or the front of the veil facing you.

To keep the first stitch from tearing the illusion, fold back a small triangle (about 1/2") at one corner of the edge to be gathered. Put the needle once through the triangle and immediately back between the two threads to form a knot that cannot escape through the holes in the illusion.

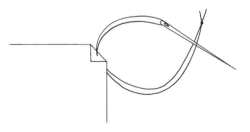

Your stitches, about 1/4" apart and 1/4" deep, will actually be made around the edge of the illusion in a spiral, pricking into the illusion at the back and emerging at the front. Moving your needle in a circular motion, take as many stitches at one time as you can pack onto the needle.

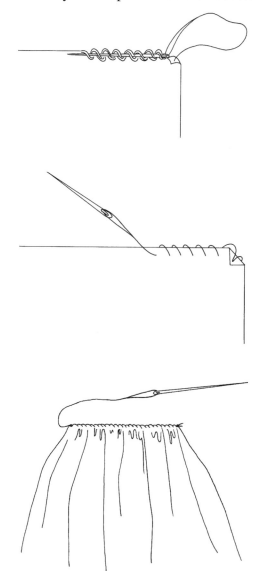

Each time the needle is filled, empty the stitches onto the length of thread and repeat the process until the entire edge is gathered.

When you have finished gathering, adjust the gathers on your length of thread until you have the measurement that will fit your headpiece. Knot and cut the thread.

GATHERING A TWO TIERED VEIL

For a two tiered veil that has been cut in one piece, gather in the same way along the creased edge of the illusion.

edge. Press the crease out of the ungathered section of the veil.

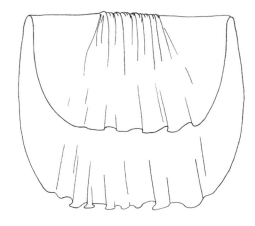

GATHERING A HEART-SHAPED VEIL

Gather the long center panel to the width of your comb or headpiece. Gather each of the two shorter side panels to one-half that width — You can gather them onto the same thread, one after the other. Center the side panels on top of the center panel, and sew them together.

NOTE: A heart-shaped veil really requires an embellished edge to define its shape—-Otherwise, it may just appear that the illusion has been accidentally torn. For help in designing your veil edging, please turn to page 45.

GATHERING A CASCADE VEIL

The two tiers of a cascade veil are also gathered along the creased edge, but the gathers do not extend all the way to the edges. Gather only the center of the crease, starting and stopping at least 18" from either

Veil Edgings

A veil with an unadorned edge gives a bride an ethereal aura, surrounding her in an airy cloud of illusion — With no defined edges, the beholder is never quite sure where it begins or ends. No edging at all, or a tiny rolled edge, is the appropriate finish if the detailing on your gown is to remain the focal point of your ensemble.

Keep your pearl and ribbon edgings small — Pearls just 2-1/2 to 3 millimeters in diameter or ribbon 1/8" wide will define the edge beautifully and are light enough to allow the illusion to maintain its buoyancy. Edging lace can be quite wide, depending on the effect desired — It can be visually heavy without physically weighting down your veil.

Edging your veil with pearls, ribbon, or monofilament is a skill that requires some practice to perfect. It is strongly recommended that you practice with scraps of illusion and trimmings to develop the right touch and to fine-tune your sewing machine settings before advancing to the veil itself.

Edge your veil while it is still flat and ungathered. The lower corners of the veil must be rounded when trimmings are being applied.

Be sure to have plenty of edging material available in one length because joins cannot be made invisibly. For a two tiered veil cut in one piece, use a separate length of edging for each tier. Be careful to sew them both to the

outside of the veil (Monofil-ament can be sewn in one piece around the two tiered veil, beginning and ending at the crease).

SERGED ROLLED HEM

A simple rolled edge defines the edge of the veil with subtlety and simplicity. Follow the instructions for your particular serger. Use normal sewing thread to keep the serged edge light and delicate, and a rolled hem rather than a narrow edge technique to keep the threads from pulling away from the edge.

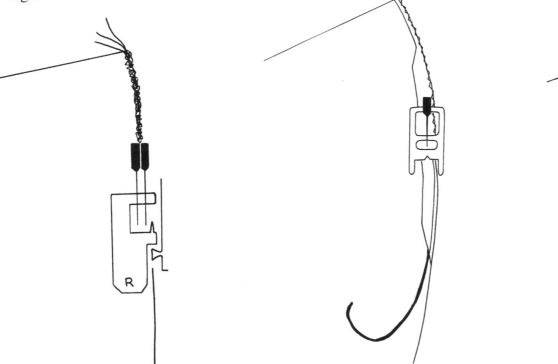

EARL COTTON

For a similar effect to the serged edge that can be sewn on a sewing machine, fold the edge of the illusion over a length of pearl cotton — a fine yarn used for tatting and crochet — and zigzag over it with a narrow stitch. Cut away the excess illusion close to the stitching. To keep the ball of yarn under control as you sew, place it in an open sewing machine drawer or in a small box on the floor.

PEARLS OR RIBBON

A specially designed pearl foot or ribbon foot for your serger or sewing machine has a groove to guide the trimmings alongside the edge of the illusion as you sew. Using one of these feet, even a novice can obtain a beautiful result with a minimum of practice.

Follow the directions for your particular machine and foot, with one exception: The illusion is too slippery to stay in place in the guide on the left side of the foot, so feed it under the entire foot instead.

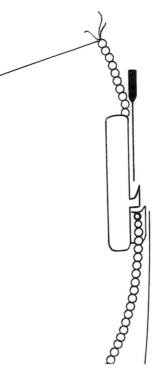

Monofilament

Monofilament is a clear thread made from a single continuous nylon fiber. Use it to give a ruffled "lettuce-leaf" edge to your veil or pouf.

For information on choosing and purchasing monofilament, please turn to page 11.

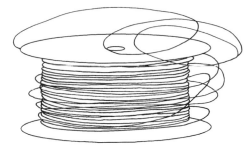

The monofilament's behavior as it is unwound from the spool might better be described as misbehavior. A stick-straight fiber has been unnaturally twisted around a cylinder, and with time has become "permed" into a spiral. Delighted in its newfound liberty, it will try to do its wild dance of freedom all around your work space. It is your

mission to squelch that particular mode of expression.

If you had three arms, the third one would be useful right now for keeping the curls of monofilament at a slight distance so they cannot get caught in your stitches. Barring that third arm, a stand for holding cones of thread, like the one on a serger, is ideal.

If you have a thread stand, place it to the right and in back of your sewing machine. Wrap a rubber band or "twistie tie" around one wire eye to turn it into a completely closed circle that will prevent the monofilament's escape. Place the spool on the stand and thread the end of the monofilament through the circle.

If no cone stand is available, place your spool of monofilament into an empty sewing machine drawer to your right.

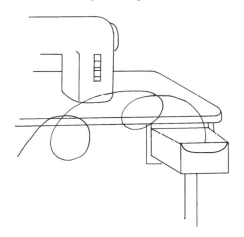

If your machine allows it, move the needle position as far to the right as possible to prevent the monofilament from jumping out of the stitches. Adjust your zigzag stitch for a medium length and width.

Begin with 2" of the monofilament hanging in back of the illusion. Keeping a grip on both, place the needle into the illusion about 2" from the corner and sew backwards over the monofilament all the way back to the corner.

As you sew, your left hand controls the tension of the illusion, your right hand the tension of the monofilament. The degree of ruffling is controlled by the ratio of illusion to monofilament. For softer ruffles, feed them together at about the same rate; for tighter ruffles, stretch the illusion as it feeds, while allowing the monofilament to flow more freely. It is important to develop a consistent tension for both materials so that the ruffling will be consistent. Sew as continuously as possible around the veil edge.

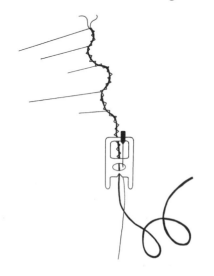

$\mathscr{L}$ACE

Position the lace over the edge of the illusion so that the decorative edge of the lace becomes the edge of the veil. The way that the lace is placed upon the edge depends upon whether the pattern of the lace you have chosen is symmetrical or asymmetrical.

To place a symmetrical lace pattern on your veil, center a lace motif at the midpoint of the lower edge and pin the lace toward the upper corners.

An asymmetrical Alencon or Venice lace may actually be fashioned from motifs that come in mirrored pairs. If so, cut the motifs apart and place them individually on the edge of the illusion, beginning at both sides of the top and working your way toward the center back. If necessary, disguise the join at the center back by an arrangement of cut motifs.

For an asymmetrical lace that cannot be cut apart, begin placing your lace at either side of the top, positioning the dominant motif at either corner.

This will give you the illusion (no pun intended!) of a symmetrically placed lace pattern. Work from both sides toward the center of the lower edge.

A single line of stitching should be sufficient to hold the lace in place. Camouflage the stitches by following the contours of the lace pattern rather than sewing in a straight line. If you wish, use invisible thread (fine monofilament) to make your stitches nearly invisible.

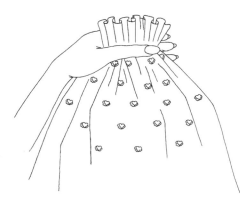

Scattered Decoration

Apply lace motifs symmetrically to your veil before it is gathered. Pearls or crystal beads may be scattered more randomly throughout the illusion, and can be applied before or after the veil is completed.

Lace

Purchase individual motifs or cut motifs from a length of lace trim or fabric. Be sure to cut around the entire motif, not through it, to avoid raveling.

Plan your design on paper or, if a large flat surface is available, lay the design out on the veil itself. Use the edges and the quarter marks where the illusion was folded onto the bolt as guides to position the appliques.

When the veil is gathered the motifs will look closer together near the gathering, so for a concentration of lace near the top that becomes sparser and ultimately fades away, you can use the same spacing throughout the veil.

Pin the appliques to the illusion. Informally gather the top of the veil with your hands to visualize the effect after the veil has been gathered, and make any necessary adjustments. Turn the veil over to allow you to glue from the wrong side.

Place a large clean sheet of white tissue paper over the work surface to absorb excess glue. As you work, a small amount of glue will inevitably seep through the motifs onto the paper, but the roughness of the paper will keep the veil in place as you work, so the glue will not be able to bleed onto clean areas of the veil. If a motif becomes stuck to the tissue paper, you can safely pry it away as long as the glue has not completely dried — any fibers from the paper that adhere to the lace will not show because they are white.

Apply white flexible glue with a "pad" formed from a scrap of illusion (about 6" x 18"). Wrap the illusion softly around itself until you have a soft ball about 2" in diameter. A pad is the perfect disposable glue applicator — The pores in the net absorb the glue, releasing just enough

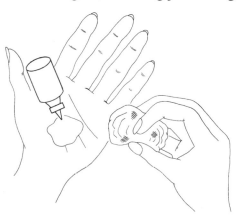

at one time to attach the lace applique without any excess to spoil the veil.

Assuming that you are right-handed, squirt a small puddle of glue directly into your left palm. With your right hand, dip the center of the pad into the puddle of glue and dab the glue onto the back of each applique, through the illusion.

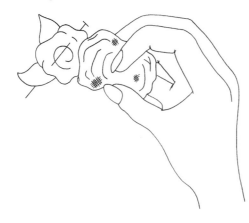

If any glue drips onto the open areas of the illusion, gently rub it out immediately with two clean pads, one placed under the illusion and the other above. The pads will quickly absorb the unwanted glue.

Remove the pins holding the appliques in place before the glue is quite dry.

𝒫EARLS

It is easiest to apply scattered individual pearls to your veil after it has been gathered.

Use a thicker white glue — such as TACKY GLUE — to keep the pearls

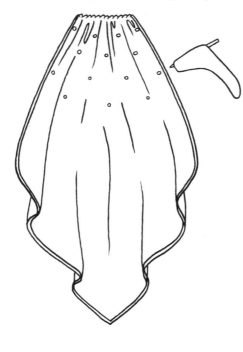

from sliding out of position under their own weight before the glue has a chance to dry.

If you can work quickly and keep the dots of glue smaller than the pearls, you can use hot glue to keep them in place. Hot glue has the advantage of drying almost instantly, allowing no chance for the objects to roll away from the illusion. The work will go much faster, especially if you are making multiple veils, and the veil will not take up your entire work space while you wait for the white glue to dry.

Instead of randomly scattering single pearls or beads, cluster 3 or more together to form miniature patterns within your all over scattering scheme. Use this technique to echo a detail from the gown, or as a focal point if the design of the gown is relatively simple. For a better result with a more precise design like this, apply the pearls while the veil is still flat.

You can use the same techniques to scatter other small trimmings into your veil — individual flower blossoms, bows, leaves, sequins, or crystal beads.

Poufs

A dainty pouf — a delicate mist of illusion at the back of your headpiece — is a lovely setting for a modest gathering of flowers or ribbons, while a more generous pouf creates a soft, flattering frame for your face.

If you're satisfied with the design of your headpiece but something about it just isn't working, try adding a small pouf — Simply reintroducing the veiling material into the body of the headpiece can unify your design, pulling all of the elements together. Suddenly, it all looks "right"!

Because of its airy, translucent quality, a pouf can add height to your headpiece without adding any height to you — If a wreath or a V-band seems too severely horizontal for you or your gown, adding a pouf may give it the lift that it needs to stop weighting you down.

The size of your pouf should be in proportion to your headpiece, your hair style, and your gown. A really huge pouf could steal focus from other design details — But, if you're looking for a simply stunning detail to be the center of attention, go for it!

Some of the construction techniques referred to in this section are more fully described in the previous sections in this unit.

THE CLOUD POUF

Floating like a puff of translucent cotton candy, a cloud pouf — with no visible raw edges — is the most ethereal style. This illustration shows a pouf used in a most unusual and dramatic way — On top of the bride's head rather than behind it.

Cut a strip of illusion 8"-18" wide and between 54" and 72" long. Round all four corners.

Fold the illusion in half lengthwise, and gather both edges together, including the rounded corners.

Arrange the gathers evenly on the thread, and cut the thread to the desired measurement.

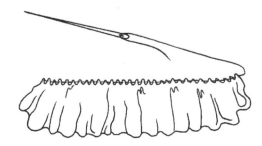

Sew the pouf to the back of your headpiece. Gently pull the two layers apart every few inches near the stitching to adjust the fullness.

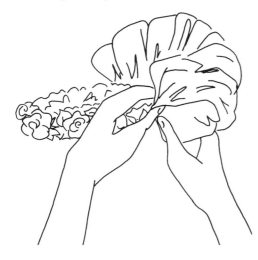

THE LOOPED POUF

A looped pouf's fullness is controlled at intervals along its width, so it holds its shape extremely well.

Begin with a strip of illusion 12"-16" wide and 54" long. Divide the length into 5 to 8 equal sections — The number of sections will affect the finished size and density of the pouf.

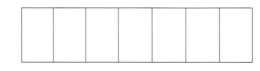

Gather the illusion at both ends and at each division as tightly as possible.

Pin the loops evenly across the back of your headpiece and sew them into place. Pull the loops apart near the gathering, and arrange the loops so that the raw edges remain hidden inside.

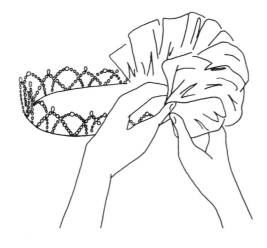

THE RUFFLED POUF

A ruffled pouf gathered down the center will stand up crisply yet softly from your headpiece.

Cut a strip of illusion 5"-10" wide by 54" long. Round all four corners, and crease the illusion lengthwise so that the edges are about 1" apart.

If you wish, you can apply pearls, monofilament, or ribbon to the edges of your pouf before gathering.

Gather along the crease, and cut your thread twice as long as your finished pouf will be. Fold both ends in to meet the center.

Sew the pouf to your headpiece, and pull the layers apart every few inches near the stitching to adjust the fullness.

Scatter pearls, sequins, or individual flowers within a pouf for a magical effect — they will appear to be suspended in midair.

Marrying Your Veil to Your Headpeice

Sewing your veil directly to your headpiece is fast and easy, and it is perfectly sensible to do that if your veil is short enough to be worn comfortably throughout the rest of your day. But attaching your veil with a narrow strip of hook and loop tape instead means that you can remove your veil without removing the entire headpiece. If you wish, you can even replace it with a shorter veil that will be more comfortable to wear while you chat and dance with your guests.

Cut a piece of hook and loop tape the length of the gathered section of your veil. Sew one side of it to your veil, and sew or glue the other side to your headpiece.

Always position the hook and loop tape where it will be hidden — Either inside of the headpiece, or tucked under a flower or piece of lace on the outside. The rougher hooked side of the tape should face away from your head to avoid becoming entangled with your hair.

HEADPIECES

Actually, it is almost redundant to refer to headpieces as "bridal" headpieces, for they have no counterpart at all in real life. (When's the last time you wore a glittering white chapeau bedecked with flowers, pearls, and a long train of illusion with another ensemble in your wardrobe?) So have fun — Your wedding day is your golden opportunity to cast aside the everyday rules governing the rest of fashion and play dress-up.

Remember — Bridal millinery is a form of sculpture, an art rather than a science. Be creative, and don't be afraid to alter the techniques described here to fit your design and your components. As long as your headpiece looks wonderful and stays together securely, you're doing things correctly!

The Beaded Tiara

A tiara fabricated from a combination of pearls and Austrian crystal beads is a regal culmination to a traditional ball gown or serene sheath dress.

Wear a tiara with a more formal hair style, never with plain straight hair or a sporty 'do (Remember how silly Princess Di's jeweled tiara looked worn over her natural hairstyle?).

A tiara should be carefully scaled to your own height and the height of the groom — This is one instance where YOUR headpiece could make HIM look shorter!

Tiara Design

Make your beaded tiara with two or more rows of loops or points joined to the same base, with a smaller design at the base as a finishing. The complexity and interest of your design increases with the number of rows, the variation of loop or point designs, and the introduction of other components around the base.

Graduate the size of your tiara's loops or points, with a larger one at the center front flanked by increasingly smaller ones at either side, so that your design leads the eye gracefully around the headpiece.

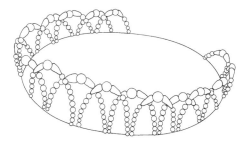

Materials

Millinery wire (approx. 2 yards)

24-gauge jewelry wire

Pearls, Austrian crystal beads

Other trimmings of your choice

2-3 yards 1/4" satin ribbon

2-3 yards 3/8" satin ribbon

3/4 yard elastic bridal loops

Combs

Hook and loop tape

Make a Base

For a plain round (oval) base, make three identical rings of millinery wire joined at the center back with either wire joiners or short lengths of jewelry wire. If you wish, bind the three rings together with jewelry wire to hold them while you work.

Beading Samples

Experiment with different combinations of pearls and Austrian crystal beads until you find several that you like. The patterns may be composed of all pearls or all beads, but a combination of pearls and beads in different sizes adds excitement.

ROUNDED LOOPS

Use 24 gauge jewelry wire, cut 6"-8" long. Before stringing any beads onto the wire, bend the wire about 1" from one end — to prevent the pearls and beads from falling off — and bend the other end in the same way when you have finished. If you wish, graduate the individual designs so that there is a larger pearl or bead at the center as a focal point.

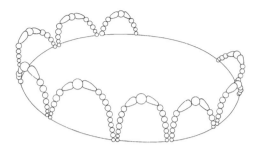

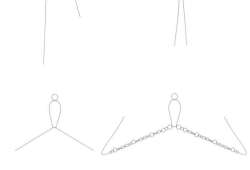

POINTS

Cut 6" lengths of 24 gauge jewelry wire. Bend the wire in half. String one tiny bead or pearl onto the center, thread BOTH ends of the wire through a large drop pearl or bead, and bend the wires in opposite directions to hold the two beads or pearls in place. String the free ends of the wire with a combination of pearls and beads, and crimp the ends to prevent their escape.

MAKE A PROTOTYPE

The only way to tell what your tiara will look like finished is to make a prototype first. At this stage, you can determine how many loops or points you need, add or delete beads to alter the height of your tiara, and adjust the spacing of the loops or points to alter its density.

From your beading samples, select the designs that you like best. Make enough samples to make a prototype of the entire tiara.

For the prototype, begin each row at the center front and work your way outward, wrapping the free ends of the wires around the base so that the ends of the points or loops just meet.

When you are satisfied with the overall size and shape of the first row, add a second row of loops or points, wrapping the wires in between the first wrappings. Add additional rows of loops and points in the same way until your design is complete.

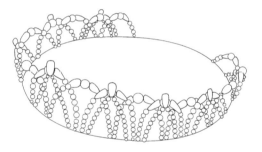

THE REAL THING

If you have enough millinery wire, pearls, and beads, it is easiest to copy your mockup while it is still intact. Should you need to reuse everything, make a schematic drawing of your design before dismantling it, using different sizes of circles for pearls and another shape like a triangle to represent beads. Don't forget to include notes on the spacing of the loops or points.

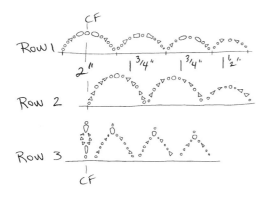

While it was easiest to construct your mockup from many short lengths of wire, to allow for fast and easy changes to any part of the design, it is actually easier to form the loops with one continuous wire. Using one wire also gives a cleaner line to the base, as there is only half as much wire being wrapped around it between loops.

Conversely, points are nearly impossible to make in one continuous length of wire, because the wire needs to double back on itself tightly in exactly the right spot in order to form a perfect point. Make and attach your points individually, just as you did for the mockup.

Cut a length of jewelry wire long enough to form all the loops in one row — Usually, 48" will do the job comfortably.

With a pencil, mark the spacing of the first row of loops or points on the base.

THE SECRET OF THE TIARA

To keep the loops and points standing up straight, one end of your wire must be located at the inside of the base and the other at the outside — The inside wire keeps the loop or point from falling forward, while the outside wire keeps it from falling back.

Wrap the wires tightly three or four times around the base.

The wires in these illustrations are shown wrapped MUCH more loosely than you will be wrapping them — Wrap the wires as closely together as you can, or even overlap them.

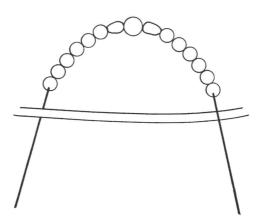

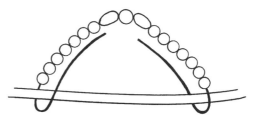

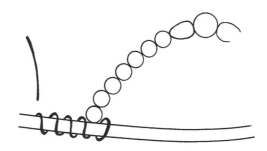

With the free end of the wire coming from behind the base, wrap one end of the jewelry wire around the base at the marking furthest to the back on the right side of the tiara. (This will mean you are working toward your right — you may wish to reverse the direction if you are left-handed.) Wrap the wire three or four times around the base, and cut off the excess.

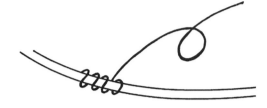

String the pattern of beads for the first loop onto the wire. Wrap the free end three or four times around the base at the second marking so that the end of your loop is at the front of the base. Crimp but do not cut the wire.

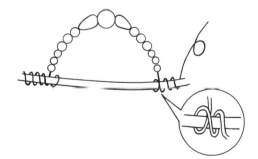

String the combination of beads and pearls for the second loop onto the wire, and repeat the process around the base. When you have completed the row, wrap the wire around the base three or four times, crimp it with the pliers, and cut it.

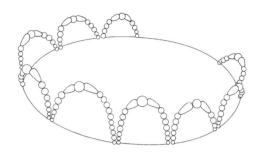

Follow the same procedure with the remaining rows until you have completed your design.

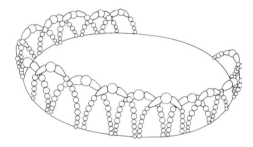

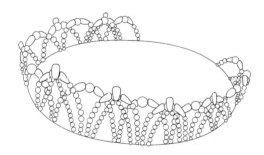

THE BASE ROW
The base row may be simply a strand of pearls or beads glued around the perimeter of the base (do that later — See page 61), or a small arrangement of beaded wire loops, silk or hand-made flowers, or pearl sprays. Whatever you choose, the base row should not overpower the overall design of your tiara.

If your design calls for beaded wire loops or flowers, construct them individually or in small groupings.

For a small loop or leaf shape, cut a 4"-6" length of jewelry wire, thread it with a pattern of pearls and beads, and twist the free ends of the wire together close to the beads.

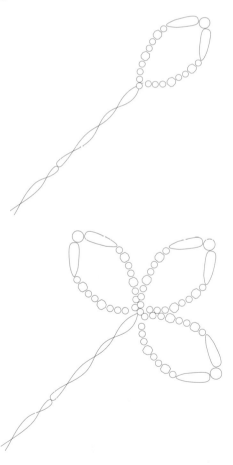

For a cluster of small loops, cut a longer length of wire. Thread it with a pattern of pearls and beads, twist the free ends together, and then repeat as many times as necessary, using the same wire and twisting the base of each new loop close to the others.

To make a beaded flower, form a cluster of 4-6 beaded loops on the same wire, twist the wire together to form a circle, and add a decorative center.

Wrap the stems of your leaves, flowers, or clusters around the base of the tiara at the desired intervals.

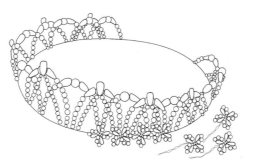

If you are adding silk or handmade flowers, pearl sprays, or other components to your base row, wire or hot glue those in place last.

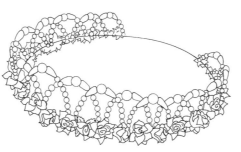

ℱINISHING

To prevent the sharp ends of the wires from scratching you, dab a bit of hot glue over them. Then, give a professional finish to the tiara by wrapping the entire base with satin ribbon.

Use 1/4" satin ribbon to wrap the beaded area of the base, because it will be easier to maneuver the narrower ribbon around all of your wires, and 3/8" satin ribbon to wrap the plain millinery wire at the back of the tiara.

Work with just one yard of ribbon at a time. You'll need more to go around the tiara, but a shorter length is more manageable and prevents tangles so the work will progress more quickly. When you do need to add length, simply hot glue the second piece of ribbon over the end of the first one and continue wrapping.

Begin wrapping at one end of the beaded section. Hot glue the end of the ribbon to the base on a slight diagonal going in the direction that

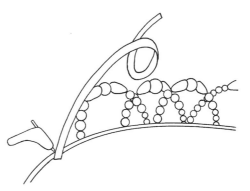

you will be working. Wrap the ribbon around the base—-Each wrapping should overlap the previous one by half the ribbon's width. Be sure the ribbon covers all of the jewelry wire, especially the sharp ends.

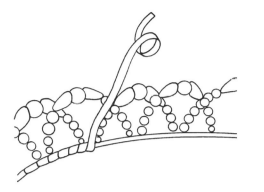

When you reach the end of the beaded section, hot glue the end of the ribbon and cut off the excess.

Wrap the 3/8" ribbon around the base at the back of the tiara in the same way.

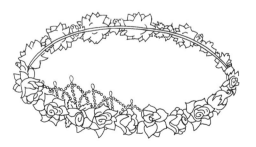

If your design calls for it, hot glue a row of pearl strands around the base after it has been finished with ribbon.

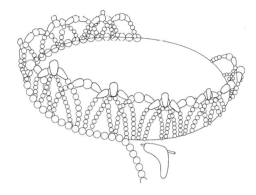

If it seems that the bumps in the base will distort the straight row of pearls, glue or sew the pearls to a length of narrow ribbon first, and then glue the ribbon to the base, pulling it smooth over the bumps.

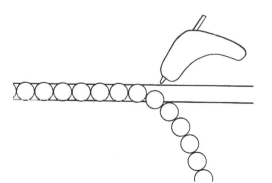

Sew or glue a length of elastic bridal loops all around the inside of the tiara. Cut a comb in half and slide the teeth through the loops on either side. For extra security, use the remaining loops for bobby pins.

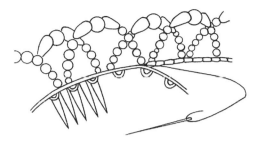

Sew your veil to the back of your tiara. If your veil will be detachable, sew a length of hook and loop tape to the back instead.

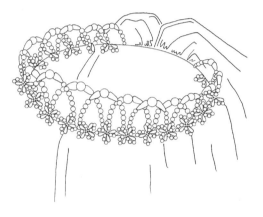

A TIARA HERE, A TIARA THERE...

As an interesting design detail, a tiara can be combined with a number of headpiece shapes to add height, dimension, and elegance. Always complete the tiara first, before finishing or decorating the remainder of the headpiece.

A wreath that seems too horizontal on its own may benefit from a small tiara added to the front, behind the flowers or other components.

At the back of a headband, a tiara is a delicate backdrop for the flowers, beads, or other components on the body of the headpiece. Make the tiara section separately on a length of millinery wire, and sew or glue it to the headband.

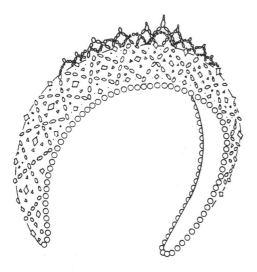

If your conservative SAF (Significant Authority Figure) is skeptical of your choice of a bridal cowboy hat, formalize it with a traditional tiara in place of a hat band — a compromise that makes you everyone's hero!

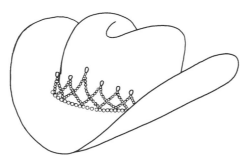

The Crown

Make a genuinely regal crown from ready-made pearl or bead sprays on wire stems. Be sure to purchase sprays that have very sturdy stems, so that the crown will hold its own shape and not be easily crushed.

Some of the techniques used in making a crown were more fully described in the previous section, THE BEADED TIARA. Please turn to pages 56-62 for more complete directions.

MATERIALS

Millinery wire (approx. 2 yards)

Pearl or bead sprays (approx. 24-36)

24 gauge jewelry wire (optional)

Pearls, Austrian crystal beads (optional)

Other trimmings of your choice

2-3 yards 1/4" satin ribbon

 2-3 yards 3/8" satin ribbon

3/4 yard elastic bridal loops

Combs

Hook and loop tape

MAKING THE CROWN

Make a base from millinery wire, following the directions on page 56.

Using your needlenose pliers, bend the wire stems of your pearl sprays at a 90-degree angle, and trim the stems to 1" beyond the bend.

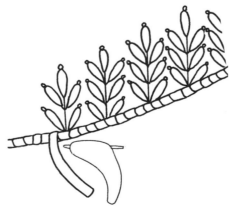

Hot glue the sprays to the base at regular intervals to insure uniform spacing.

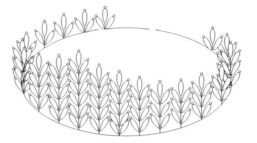

If you wish, combine one or more rows of loops or points with your vertical sprays (Refer back to page 56). Work the loops or points first, then add the sprays.

Add a base row, then wrap the base with ribbon as described on page 60.

FINISHING

Sew or glue a length of elastic bridal loops all around the inside of the crown. Cut a comb in half and slide the teeth through the loops on either side. For extra security, use the remaining loops for bobby pins.

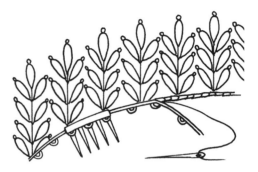

If your veil is to be detachable, sew a piece of hook and loop to the back of the frame. Or, you can sew your veil directly to the headpiece.

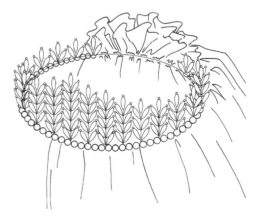

The Lace Tiara

In the bridal industry, the words "crown" or "tiara" are often used to describe a variety of styles that are actually wire frames, headbands, or wreaths, but have the look of a tiara. A lace tiara is actually a marriage between two headpiece styles — a tiara and a wire frame.

MATERIALS

Plain wire tiara frame

24 gauge jewelry wire

Pearls, Austrian crystal beads

Horsehair braid

Lace motifs

Other trimmings of your choice

2-3 yards 3/8" satin ribbon

3/4 yard elastic bridal loops

Combs

Hook and loop tape

A REGAL BEGINNING

Purchase a plain wire frame — one with NO horsehair already applied — in any of a number of available tiara shapes.

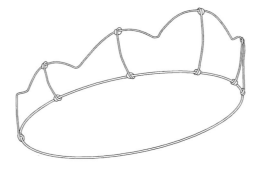

Add loops or points to the top edge of the frame, using the methods described in THE BEADED TIARA, page 56. Keep this tiara section relatively tiny, to keep your headpiece from being too tall. To reduce bulk, dab a little hot glue over the sharp ends of the jewelry wire but do not wrap the wire frame with ribbon.

Cover the outside of the wire frame with horsehair braid using the principles described in THE JULIET CAP, page 70.

If you're not adding loops or points to the top of you lace tiara, you can purchase a frame that is covered in horsehair and begin your construction at this point.

LACE MOTIFS & TRIMMINGS

Cut several sizes of individual motifs from Alencon or Venice lace. To make the motifs bendable, form loops of soft millinery wire and use white flexible glue to adhere them to the backs of the motifs.

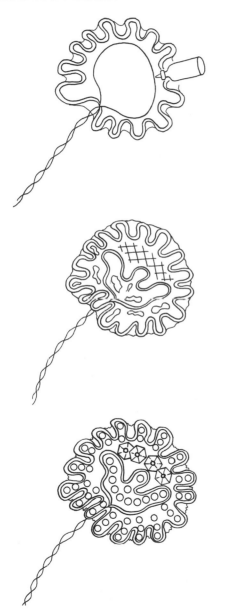

Even if the lace was purchased already beaded, you will probably wish to add additional pearls or clear sequins, to lend the motifs more substance.

Arrange the largest motifs on the frame, folding any excess under the bottom edge of the frame. Glue them to the horsehair with white flexible glue.

Once the white glue has dried, build up the smaller motifs in layers, using hot glue, to form a three-dimensional design. For a more interesting and complex design, include other components as well — Pearls, beads, or flowers.

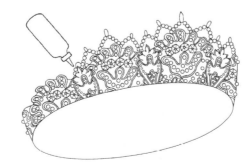

Shape the wires at the backs of the motifs to enhance your design.

Finishing

If your frame has exposed millinery wire at the back, wrap it with 3/8" satin ribbon.

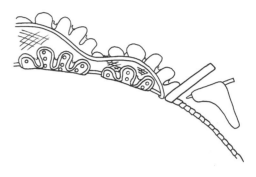

Sew or glue a length of elastic bridal loops all around the inside of the tiara. Cut a comb in half and slide the teeth through the loops on either side. For extra security, use the remaining loops for bobby pins.

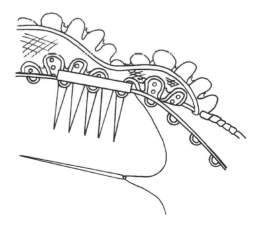

For a detachable veil, sew a length of hook and loop tape to the back of your tiara frame. You can also sew your veil directly to the headpiece.

The Headband

Whether your hair is tightly curled, stick-straight, as long as Rapunzel's, or gamin-short, your sparkling eyes and radiant expression take center stage when your hair is held softly back and away from your face with a flattering headband.

A headband is a simple traditional or contemporary look that is among the easiest headpieces to wear. Most brides wear a headband with natural or loosely styled hair — If your hair will be worn more formally for your wedding, keep it soft rather than sleek so that the effect will not be too severe. Or, for a more regal look, try tipping your headband on its side — almost like a tiara — to wear it with a more sophisticated upswept 'do.

A Padded Headband Frame

Use a ready-made padded headband frame covered in satin as a base for your headband. The slight padding

gives the headband just enough dimension to allow it to be seen from the front, without disappearing completely into your hair or adding much height. The padding also gives you something to sew into if you will be beading your headband.

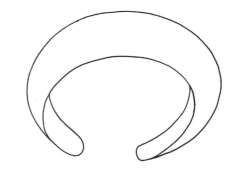

If you cannot find a ready-made frame, you can easily pad and cover one yourself.

Materials

Unpadded plastic headband frame

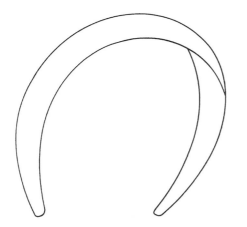

Soft foam padding (1/2" or 3/4" thick and the length and width of the headband)

1/4 yard fabric for the covering

1/4 yard satin ribbon, a little narrower than the headband

Trimmings of your choice

1/8 yard elastic bridal loops

Padding Your Frame

Hot glue the foam to the top of the headband, then trim it to size. There is no need to round

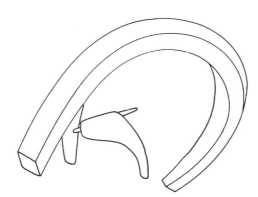

off the corners of the foam, because the fabric covering will "smoosh" the foam into shape all by itself.

Cut a piece of fabric — on the bias — approximately 3" wide and 15" long.

Place the fabric over the headband and hot glue the edges of the fabric to the inside, pleating in the excess at either end.

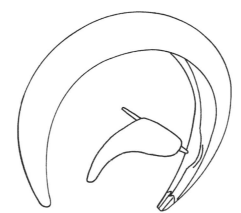

Turn under the ends of the satin ribbon and glue it to the inside of the headband to cover the raw edges of the fabric.

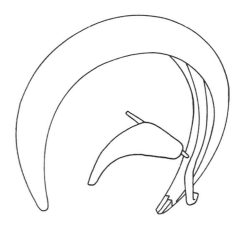

If you wish, glue a length of elastic bridal loops to the inside of the back of your headband and use them for bobby pinning.

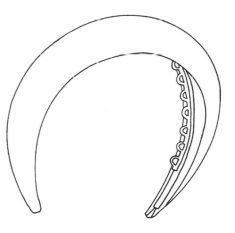

HEADBAND TRIMMINGS

If you wish, cover a purchased padded headband frame with another layer of fabric to match your gown, following the directions above.

Decorate your padded headband with a pattern of pearls and Austrian crystal beads in

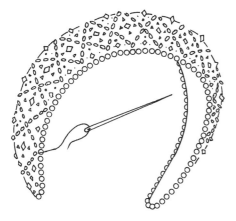

several different sizes and shapes. It is easier to sew these in place than to glue them — and, if you want to change or improve your design, you can do it easily by clipping your threads and starting again.

To add height and elegance, include a small beaded tiara at the back of your headband — Construct the tiara separately on a length of millinery wire, then sew or glue it to the back of the headband (For directions on making tiaras, turn to page 56).

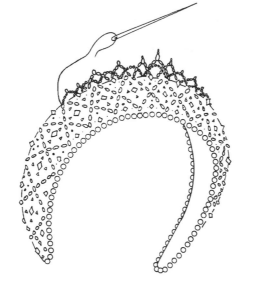

For a more three-dimensional quality, include silk or handmade flowers and pearl leaves in your design. For an asymmetrical look, let the flowers and pearls extend down further on one side.

Sew your veil directly to the back of the headband, or use a piece of hook and loop tape instead if your veil is to be detachable.

A Buckram Headband

If your design requires a wider headband — 2"-3" wide — cover a buckram headband frame with fabric to match your gown.

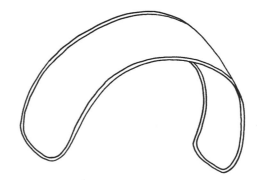

Covering a buckram headband frame is very much like making a hat, so please read the HATS unit starting on page 86, before you begin.

ATERIALS

Buckram frame

1/4 yard each cotton flannel, fashion fabric, and lace lining

Trimmings of your choice

1/8 yard elastic bridal loops

Comb

AKE A PATTERN

To make a pattern, trace around the outer edge of the frame, then add 1-1/2" all around. Cut one each from your fashion fabric, flannel, and lining.

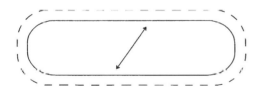

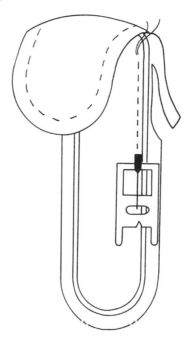LANNEL COVERING

Center the flannel on the frame. Stitch it by hand or by machine to the edge of the frame just inside the wire. Clip the seam allowance to 1/4".

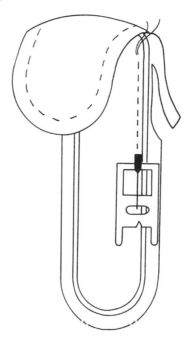ABRIC COVERING

Pin your fashion fabric to the frame, turning the seam allowance under the edges.

If your headpiece design includes an edging — lace, pearls, etc — around the headband that will hide the stitches, sew through the right side, the frame, and the turned under edge. Do this step by hand so your machine's

mechanism cannot mar your fashion fabric.

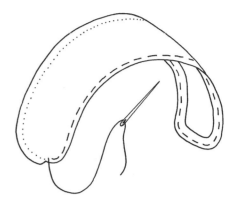

If there is to be no edging around the headband, pin under the seam allowance and hot glue it to the inside of the frame.

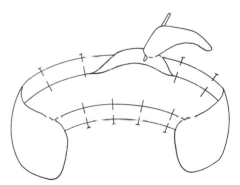

Clip away the excess seam allowance.

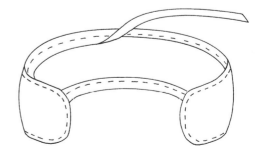

ℒINING

Hot glue the center of the lace lining to the top inside of the frame to keep it in place.

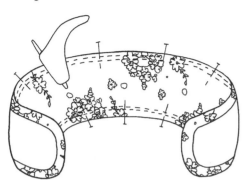

Hot glue the edges of the lining to the seam allowance of the fashion fabric, gluing right through the lace to the fabric.

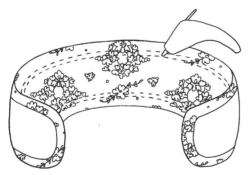

Clip away the excess seam allowance and hot glue a narrow (1/4" – 3/8") edging lace over the raw edge of the lining.

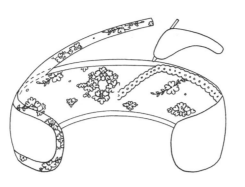

ℱINISHING

Sew a comb to the inside of your headband, or glue a length of elastic bridal loops to the lining and slip the comb's teeth through the loops.

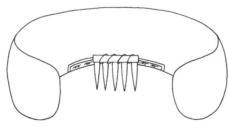

Sew your veil to the back of the headband. If your veil is to be detachable, sew or glue a length of hook and loop tape to the underside of the back of the headband.

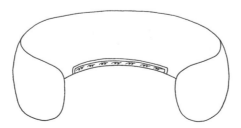

The Juliet Cap

Shaped to nestle tranquilly at the crest of your head, the classically simple Juliet cap has remained popular ever since its introduction in Medieval times. The Juliet cap is a true chameleon — The same shape looks completely different when worn with a long, flowing hairstyle and a simple homespun gown than it does perched upon a sophisticated upswept coif with a heavily beaded silk ball gown and a cathedral-length train.

Your Juliet cap may have a frame made of millinery wire or buckram. Choose a wire frame for a lighter, more translucent headpiece that will be finished in no time, or a buckram frame if you want to cover your Juliet cap with fabric to match your gown.

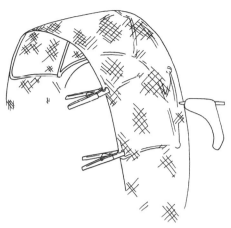

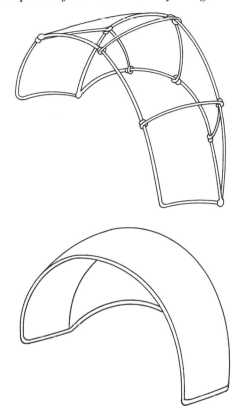

To cover a buckram Juliet cap frame, follow the directions for covering a buckram headband frame, found on page 68.

THE WIRE FRAME

For a quick and easy finished headpiece, start with a wire frame, and decorate your Juliet cap with lace appliques.

Although it is possible to cleverly arrange and glue lace appliques or flowers directly over a bare wire frame to hide the millinery wire, using a frame covered with horsehair braid provides a more solid surface for your embellishments and allows you to place them in between the wires.

If possible, purchase a wire frame already covered with horsehair braid. Or, cover a plain wire frame with horsehair yourself.

MATERIALS

Wire Juliet cap frame, plain or covered with horsehair

Horsehair braid (optional)

Lace appliques

Trimmings of your choice

1/4 yard elastic bridal loops

Comb

ADDING A HORSEHAIR COVERING

Choose a horsehair braid wide enough to cover the entire frame in one piece, and work with a strip several inches longer than the frame. Hold the horsehair to the frame with spring clip clothespins or straight pins.

Working in small sections from the right side, apply hot glue liberally through the horsehair to the edges of the frame. While the glue is still hot, press the horsehair to the frame (using a spare glue stick to prevent burning your fingers) to strengthen the bond.

Carefully clip away the excess horsehair close to the wire. Believe it or not — You're almost finished!

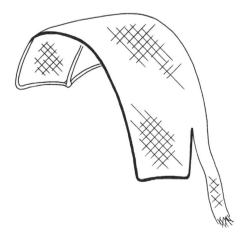

EMBELLISHMENTS

Use a white flexible glue to adhere lace appliques, pearls, etc. to the horsehair (Don't use hot glue — it melts the nylon horsehair. That was a plus while you were bonding the horsehair to the edges of the frame, but in the larger open areas it would disintegrate your headpiece). Hold the components in place with clothes-pins or straight pins, and be sure to remove the pins before the glue has dried completely.

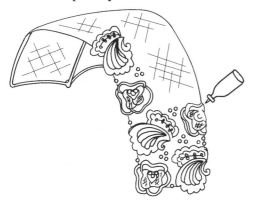

FINISHING

Sew a comb directly to the inside of the front edge of your headpiece, or glue a length of elastic bridal loops to the inside of the front edge of your Juliet cap and slip the comb's teeth through the loops. Use the remaining elastic loops for bobby pins.

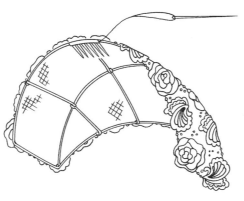

Sew your veil to the back of your headpiece. If your veil is to be detachable, sew a piece of hook-and-loop tape there instead.

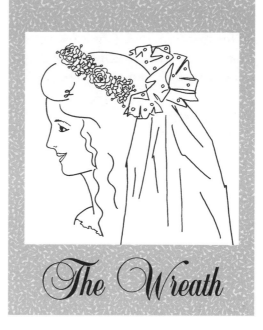

The Wreath

A wreath is such a basic headpiece shape that many brides and milliners tend to overlook its enormous design potential. The options for combining materials are endless — For example, you might consider blending silk flow-ers with pearl sprays and leaves, or substituting handmade flowers of fab-ric, ribbon, or Alencon lace. A stun-ning contemporary variation might not include flowers at all, featuring instead only pearl sprays or other components.

A simple wreath of white, ivory, or mul-ticolored flowers worn with a natural hair style is a fitting complement to a romantic country frock — And the same wreath is a magnificent and whimsical surprise when juxtaposed with an elegant silk ball gown.

Wear your wreath as it flatters you and your hair style — encircling your head, perched squarely on top of your head, or placed slightly back.

ℳ ATERIALS

Purchased wreath frame

OR

3/4 yard millinery wire

3/4 yard horsehair tubing

Flower sprays

Trimmings of your choice

3-4 yards 3/8" satin ribbon

3/4 yard elastic bridal loops

Combs

1/4 yard hook and loop tape

𝒯 HE WREATH FRAME

Use a purchased wreath frame, made from a length of millinery wire covered in horsehair tubing with the ends twisted together at the back to form a circle.

Wreath frame sizes vary among manufacturers, so ask before you order to be sure the wreath will fit as you envisioned. If the wreath is to fit around your head, allow an extra inch in the circumference to allow for the thickness of the wrapping ribbon.

Or, fashion a frame yourself from millinery wire and tubular horsehair: Cut a length of each 4" larger than the desired finished size. Mark 2" in from either end of the wire. Insert the wire into the tubing. Matching the markings, twist the free ends together and

wrap the remaining wire tightly over the circle.

In its raw state, the twisted area looks impossibly clumsy and lumpy, but the lumps disappear as the frame is wrapped with ribbon and flowers.

If you intend to position your wreath on top of your head, the frame's circular shape will do nicely, but if it is to encircle your head — which is more oval-shaped — gently squeeze in at both sides of the frame to form an oval that feels secure and fits comfortably.

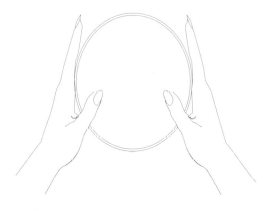

ℰ MBELLISHMENTS

Work out the design of your wreath before you begin assembly. The number of silk flowers you will need varies with your design and the size of the flowers and the wreath frame. On average, estimate five to seven flower sprays, two short wreath sprays, or one long wreath spray per headpiece.

Pearl sprays or other components can be taped into your flower sprays or incorporated individually. Angle your pearl sprays correctly now, as you will not be able to bend or twist them later.

For more information on handling flower sprays, please turn to page 20.

Flower sprays should be evenly spaced, overlapping each other with no gaps in between. Hold the flower sprays in place on the frame temporarily with small lengths of floral tape or jewelry wire.

 INISHING

When you are satisfied with your design, wrap the entire frame with satin ribbon to permanently secure your embellishments. Begin and end your wrapping at the back of the wreath.

Work with just one yard of ribbon at a time. More will be needed to go around your wreath, but a shorter length is more manageable and prevents tangles. When you need more length, simply hot glue the second piece of ribbon over the end of the first one and continue wrapping. All ribbon joins should occur on the outside of the wreath where they will be completely hidden by the flowers.

To begin wrapping, hot glue one end of the ribbon to the wreath frame on a slight diagonal in the direction that you will be working.

Wrap the ribbon around the frame, covering the stems of the floral sprays. Each time the ribbon wraps around the wreath, it should cover the previous wrapping by half the ribbon's width.

To finish wrapping, overlap your starting point by at least 1/2". Hot glue the end of the ribbon and cut off the excess.

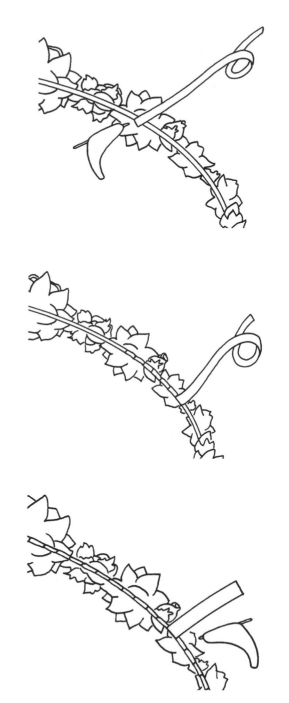

Sew or glue a length of elastic bridal loops to the inside of your wreath. Cut a comb in half, and slip the teeth through the loops at either side. Use the remaining loops for bobby pins. Sew your veil to the back of your wreath, or substitute a piece of hook and loop tape if the veil is to be detachable.

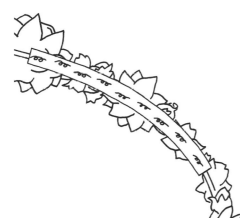

CONTROLLING THE FLOWERS

Decide how far from the frame you would like each flower to lie, and include its stem in the ribbon just enough to control its

location. Then, push that flower out of your way and begin wrapping the stem of the next flower.

Observe that if the ribbon is wound all the way up to a flower's head, the flower remains secured tight to the form, keeping it in place but allowing no natural movement away from the center. If all your flowers are wrapped that way, the result will be a very tight and narrow wreath. On the other hand, if too much of the flower's stem is left free of the ribbon, the blossom becomes "wild" and may wander away from the rest of your design.

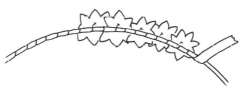

Do not be distressed to notice that the position of the flowers becomes distorted as you work. As long as you have left the proper amount of stem wire

exposed, you will be able to easily bend and twist the wire stems back to their original perfect formation.

The Cascade

A lush arrangement of silk or hand-made flowers framing your face, accented with a heavenly abundance of pearl sprays — What could possibly be more breathtakingly feminine!

Design your cascade as a bouquet of flowers for your hair. If you wish, include some of the same types of flowers that will be used in your bouquet, or use scraps of fabric from your gown to make handmade flowers.

To show your cascade at its best, surround it with a halo of soft feminine curls. Whether your hair will be worn up or down, curls really are essential — This is just not a style that can work with straight hair.

As a rule of thumb, let the degree of fullness in your cascade be proportional to the fullness in your skirt — A very full ball gown can balance a larger cascade than a short tailored suit.

ATERIALS

Purchased wreath frame

OR

3/4 yard millinery wire

3/4 yard horsehair tubing

Flowers, pearl sprays, trimmings of your choice

Floral tape

3-4 yards 3/8" satin ribbon

1/2 yard elastic bridal loops

Comb

1/4 yard hook and loop tape

MAKE A FRAME

Take a look at the photographs of cascades in the bridal magazines. Notice that many do not show the veil coming directly out of the back of the cascade — Rather, the veils and poufs are located farther back on the models' heads. The separation keeps the headpiece looking soft and feminine, so that even a fairly large cascade is not overwhelming.

To keep the cascade separate from the veil, use a purchased wreath frame or make one yourself, following the directions on page 73.

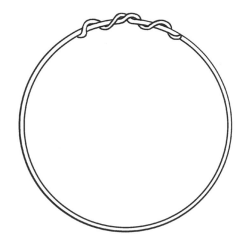

Bend the circular wire frame at an angle at either side. Try the frame on, and adjust the size of the circle and the placement of the angle until it takes the shape that you want and feels comfortable on your head.

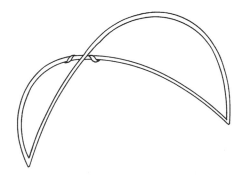

Even if your floral design is asymmetrical, bend the frame symmetrically, so that the veil lies correctly.

MBELLISHMENTS

Hold your floral sprays, pearl sprays, and other components temporarily to the front of the frame with hot glue, jewelry wire, or floral tape.

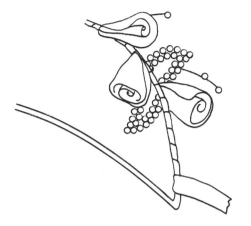

If you wish, make your design asymmetrical — Let part of the arrangement extend down longer on one

side, so that it just caresses your ear or the side of your face. Be sure that the stems of the extending flowers are secured to the frame with floral tape, wire, or hot glue. Wrap any exposed stems with satin ribbon.

ꟻINISHING

To permanently secure your embellishments to the frame and give a professional finish to your headpiece, wrap, the entire frame with satin ribbon, following the directions in the section "THE WREATH", page 74.

Sew or glue elastic bridal loops around the inside of the front of your headpiece and secure it to your hair with several half-combs or bobby pins placed through the loops.

Sew your veil to the back of the frame, or sew hook and loop tape to the frame instead if your veil is to be detachable.

A Front-Only Cascade

If your cascade design is delicate enough, or if you can use the extra height, you may want to consider having your veil come directly out of the back of your headpiece, rather than separating the two elements as was just described.

In that case, make a smaller frame from a 21" length of millinery wire. Straighten the wire and bend in 6" from either end, crimping the corners with your needle nose pliers and overlapping the free ends of the wire. Bend your frame to a shape that comfortably fits the contour of the top of your head.

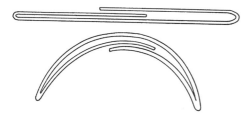

Following the directions already given, secure your floral sprays, pearl sprays, and other components to the frame with floral tape and then wrap the entire frame with ribbon.

Sew or glue elastic bridal loops to the inside of the frame and slip the teeth of a comb through the loops, or sew a comb directly to the ribbon-wrapped headpiece frame.

Sew your veil directly to the back of the headpiece frame, or substitute a length of hook and loop tape if your veil is to be detachable.

The V-band or Halo

A variation on the familiar flower wreath, the slender V-band or halo is worn around your head, just skimming your hairline or slightly below it. While the line of a halo travels in a straight horizontal line across your forehead, a V-band dips down into a graceful V at the center front.

It can be understated and romantic with a traditional full ball gown — Or outrageous and exotic, fabulous with a contemporary sheath, miniskirt, or mermaid style.

Its horizontal shape adds no height, unless of course you decide that it should — A dazzling tiara or a cloud-

like pouf at the back interrupt the horizontal lines with a more vertical shape, and keep it from visually weighting you down.

When you first try on a V-band, carefully check its effect on your facial features — While most brides can wear this style with no problem at all, the pointed shape of the center front could tend to over-emphasize closely-set eyes or a prominent nose.

Make a circle

The V-band — with its characteristic "V" shape at the center front — and the halo — a thin, even band of beads traveling straight across your forehead — are among the easiest and quickest headpieces to make. The secret is to purchase the ornately beaded front band ready-made.

Materials

Purchased beaded band

Millinery wire, jewelry wire (optional)

Trimmings of your choice

2-3 yards 3/8" satin ribbon

1/2 yard elastic bridal loops

Combs

1/4 yard hook and loop tape

The beaded band

Form a circle of the beaded band — twist the two free ends together, or overlap and fasten them with jewelry wire.

If the band is too small for your head, expand it by adding a length of millinery wire at the center back.

Since the shape of your head is not round but oval, press the circle in at the sides to form a comfortable and secure shape.

Doesn't it look impressive? The amazing part is — You're almost finished!

Trimmings

Follow the directions in the previous section — "THE WREATH" — to add flowers, pearl sprays, or other components to the sides and back of the V-band.

For an asymmetrical look, arrange a fall of flowers and pearl sprays to softly caress one side of your face. Be sure that the stems are securely taped or wired to the frame.

Finishing

Wrap the sides and back of the band with ribbon, following the directions in the previous section — "THE WREATH", page 74. Continue wrapping the ribbon over the beaded band if you have placed flowers over part of it, and and wrap the exposed stems of your asymmetrical fall with ribbon.

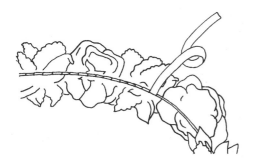

Sew or glue a length of elastic bridal loops to the inside of the wrapped section of the band. Cut a comb in half, slide the comb's teeth through the loops on either side, and use the remaining loops for bobby pins.

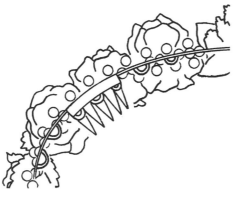

Sew your veil directly to the back of your headpiece. If it is to be detachable, sew a length of hook and loop tape there instead.

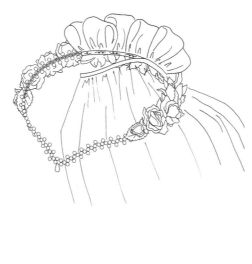

Sweet Nothings

COMBS, BARRETTES, AND BANANA CLIPS

Does a big important headpiece like a tiara or a cascade seem too overstated and oversized for your gown, your personality, or the style of your wedding?

Perhaps you were hoping for a classically simple headpiece — A headpiece that is lightweight and comfortable, that can't make you look taller, shorter, wider, or like your eyes are too close together. A headpiece design that is completely foolproof, that goes with such a variety of gowns and hair styles that it looks fabulous on just about everyone.

A decorated barrette, comb, or banana clip sounds like the perfect solution for you!

The Comb

Use a comb to support a small cascade, a medium-sized bow, or a length of plain illusion.

A SMALL CASCADE

Compose a charming design of silk or handmade flowers. Add pearl sprays, ribbons, a small pouf, or other components as you wish.

Materials

Silk or handmade flowers or sprays

Trimmings of your choice

1-2 yards 3/8" satin ribbon

Comb

Assemble YOUR TRIMMINGS

Using floral tape to fasten them together, form sprays from your flowers, pearl sprays, and other components. (For more information on working with silk flowers, please turn to page 20).

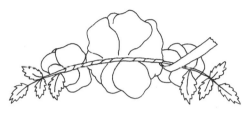

To give yourself a more solid base for sewing your comb and veil to the headpiece, wrap the main stems of your assembled cascade with several thicknesses of satin ribbon — Hot glue one end of the satin ribbon to the center of the section of stems you intend to wrap. Wrap the ribbon around the stems, doubling back and covering the entire area at least twice. When you have finished, hot glue the end of the ribbon and cut off the excess.

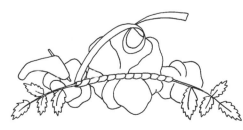

Sew your veil to the ribbon base. If your veil is to be detachable, sew a piece of hook and loop tape to the base instead.

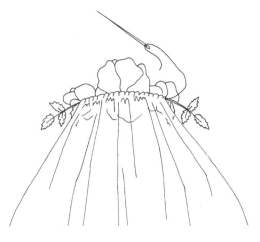

Sew a comb directly to the back of it your headpiece above the veil, taking one stitch between each of the comb's teeth.

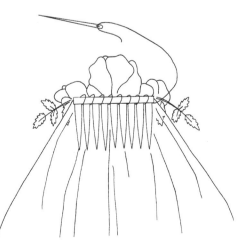

A BEAUTIFUL BOW

An unadorned bow in fabric to match your gown is a subtle declaration of understated grace. A soft or tailored bow also makes a wonderful background for a small arrangement of flowers or other components.

MATERIALS

A bow

Trimmings of your choice

Comb

EMBELLISH YOUR BOW

Make a bow to match or complement your gown (for directions, turn to page 30). For a matching bow, order extra dress fabric, ask your dressmaker for scraps, or purchase matching ribbon, tulle, or maline.

Glue or sew a cluster of flowers, pearl sprays, or other components in place over the center of your bow before completing the center knot. Or, add a glamorous button to the center of your finished bow.

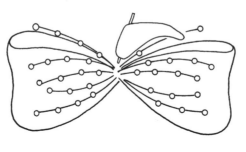

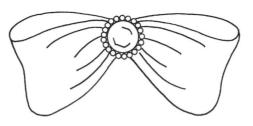

Sew your veil (or hook and loop tape, for a detachable veil) to the back of your bow.

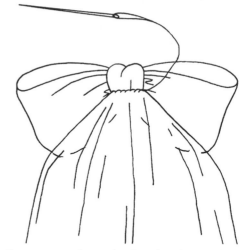

Sew a comb to the back of your bow above the veil, taking one stitch between each of the comb's teeth.

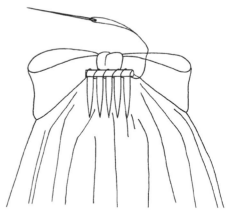

To secure a large bow, use two combs, one on either side of the knot.

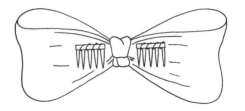

PLAIN VEILING

An unadorned length of plain veiling allows the detailing of your gown and your radiant face to take center stage. The plain veil works best with an elegantly upswept hairstyle that needs no further adornment.

MATERIALS

Bridal illusion

Comb

GATHER YOUR VEIL

Gather the top edge of your illusion to 3", to fit the width of a comb. (for directions, turn to page 43). If you are using a half-comb, gather the illusion to 1-1/2".

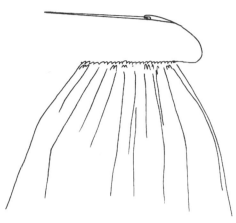

Sew the illusion directly to the comb, taking one stitch between each of the comb's teeth.

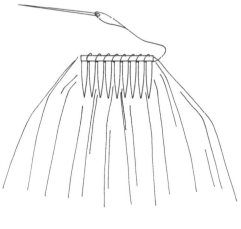

The Barrette

A barrette is especially lovely with a less formal hair style. Whether your hair is straight or curled, use the barrette to sweep a bit of hair away from your face, fastening it at the side or at the crest of your head. You can even use a barrette to hold all of your hair in a "ponytail" at the nape of your neck.

MATERIALS

Barrette

Double-stick foam tape

Trimmings of your choice

WORKING WITH THE BARRETTE

Assemble your headpiece design — an arrangement of silk or handmade flowers, a bow with pearl sprays, or any other small design that will not be too big or too heavy for the barrette.

Fasten a small piece of double-stick foam tape to the inside of the barrette — The foam will grip your hair and help the barrette to stay in place.

If the barrette has a series of perforations along its back, your headpiece can be sewn directly to it. If not, make a small base of fabric-covered buckram and glue or sew it to your barrette.

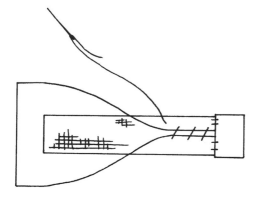

When gluing anything directly to the metal barrette, dribble a little of the hot glue inside so that it forms a continuous wrap around the edge, so even if the glue pulls away it will not dislodge the headpiece.

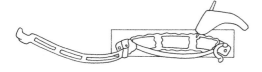

Next, sew your veil to the edge of the base. If your veil is to be detachable, sew a piece of hook and loop tape to the base instead.

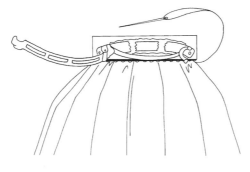

Finally, sew or glue your headpiece into position.

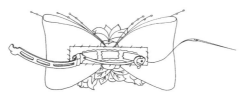

A BARRETTE BOW

For a headpiece that is easy to wear and quick to finish, sew bow loops directly to a barrette.

MATERIALS

1 1/4 yards 4" ribbon

Barrette

FASHION THE BOW

Cut a length of 4" ribbon 45" long. Divide and mark the ribbon at these intervals: 8" – 6.5" – 5" – 6" – 5" – 6.5" – 8".

| 7.5" | 6.5" | 5" | 6" | 5" | 6.5" | 7.5" |

Gather the ribbon at both ends and at each marking as tightly as possible. Sew or glue the gathered ribbon directly to your barrette. This makes a very full and soft bow, with no bulk at the center.

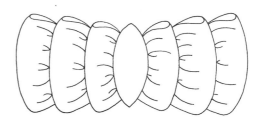

The Banana Clip

A banana clip performs a dual function — While it secures your headpiece firmly in place, it holds your lovely long hair in a romantic arrangement of luxuriously soft curls.

Materials

Banana clip

1" hook and loop tape, cut to just 1/4" in width

Trimmings of your choice

Designing Your Banana Clip

For extra security, attach an "insurance clasp" of hook and loop tape to the outside of the banana clip's clasp. Sew a 1" length of 1/4" hook and loop tape to either side of the clasp, the soft portion on one side and the rough portion on the other. Once your banana clip is closed, bring one side of the hook and loop tape over the other, just in case the plastic does not hold the clip together well enough.

Assemble your headpiece design — Accentuate the banana clip's long vertical sides with a romantic graduated arrangement of flowers, or a fluid and graceful line of rhinestones or pearls.

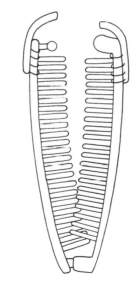

Sew your veil (or hook and loop tape, for a detachable veil) and your headpiece directly to the banana clip, taking one stitch between each tooth.

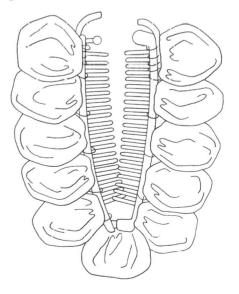

H ATS

Not long ago, a lady was not considered fully dressed unless she was wearing a hat. And not just any hat — The one that had been specially designed by her personal dressmaker to be worn with that one particular gown.

Today, it takes more than just a special occasion for most of us to wear a hat. So why be timid? On your wedding day, you're already planning to wear a dress that's quite different from your usual attire — Take advantage of this golden opportunity to pull out all the stops!

A lot of women think they don't look good in hats — Most have never really given a hat a chance. Try on several styles just to see, and don't forget that your hair and makeup will be more elaborate than usual on the day of your wedding.

CHOOSING A HAT

Depending upon the shape and the trimmings, a hat can be formal or informal, tailored or romantic, traditional or contemporary. Any hat shape may be successfully used as a bridal headpiece — a smart pillbox or cocktail hat, a chic 1920's cloche, or even a showy cowboy hat.

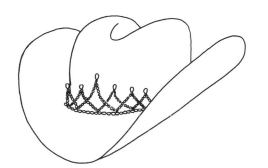

For a quick-and-easy headpiece, purchase a ready-to-trim hat in straw, felt, or horsehair from a millinery supplier.

You may also find a wonderful hat for your wedding in a department store or hat shop. The hat will probably need retrimming, so try to look beyond any trimmings to the shape and color of the hat itself — You should be able to remove any existing trimmings and add the ones you want instead.

Straw hats in white or natural are lovely for Victorian or garden weddings. Because of their beautiful texture, keep any additional ornamentation to a minimum. Trimmings should be naive and unsophisticated, in keeping with the natural character of the straw. You may wish to add some color to your straw hat — Silk wildflowers, or ribbons to match the bridesmaids' dresses.

Felt hats are not used very often for bridal wear, but can be sensational for a winter wedding. Specialty

items like cowboy hats and top hats may be made of felt, and there are some interesting felt cocktail hats on the market as well.

Trimmings on a felt hat should be bold and sophisticated — A large horsehair flower, a wide band of moire ribbon, or a scattering of pearl motifs are big enough to balance the heavier weight of the hat.

HAT FRAMES

BUCKRAM HAT FRAMES

For most hats, you will be working with a purchased buckram frame, which provides a solid foundation for your fabrics and trimmings. Buckram is a loosely woven cotton fabric impregnated with a water-soluble paste. Under steam and pressure, the headpiece shapes are machine stamped from flat sheets of buckram, then finished with an edging of millinery wire.

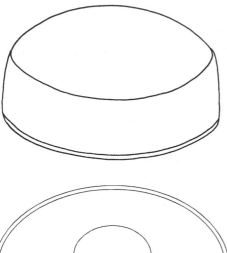

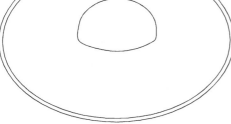

SATIN COVERED BUCKRAM FRAMES

Satin frames are marketed as "semi-finished headpieces", requiring only your trimmings and a veil to finish them, and many commercial headpiece manufacturers do use them in that way. But YOU should only use a satin frame if the entire surface will be hidden by lace, flowers, or another covering fabric Otherwise, start with a plain buckram frame and cover it with cotton flannel. Here's why —

In the manufacturing process, a layer of buckram and a layer of satin are stamped into shape together, and the two materials become laminated. The edges are wired, then bound with grosgrain ribbon. An unfortunate consequence of the manufacturing technique is that the pattern of the buckram's uneven open weave is pressed into the satin, replacing its characteristic sleekness with a pebbly, waffle-weave texture.

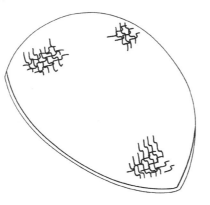

Instead of having a smooth, finished appearance, most satin-covered frames look makeshift and cheap. They are a timesaver, however, if you want to eliminate the flannel covering (see below) and proceed directly to covering your hat with fabric.

Fabrics

Cover your hat frame with fabrics and lace to match or complement your gown. Most bridal salons will be happy to order matching fabrics and lace for you.

You will be using several different fabrics in the construction of a hat — The words "fashion fabric" are used to describe the pretty fabric that is seen on the outside of your finished hat.

If you are using a lace overlay, pin the lace to the underlying fashion fabric and treat both fabrics as one unit.

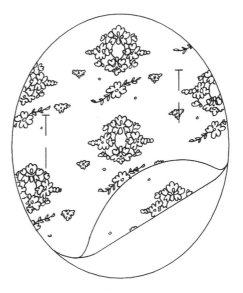

Use straight pins or spring clothespins to hold the fabric in place as you sew or glue.

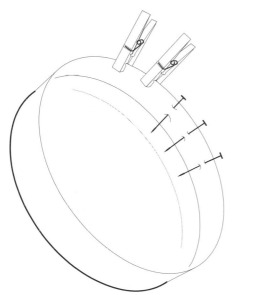

China silk and lightweight rayon are ideal linings for hats — they are easier to work with than polyester, and they mold easily to the shape of the hat. Line smaller hats with inexpensive nylon or polyester lace.

COTTON FLANNEL

For a luxurious, couture-quality result, cover a plain buckram frame with the secret ingredient of professional milliners — cotton baby flannel — before covering it with your fashion fabric.

The flannel's soft fuzzy nap smoothes out the bumps and irregularities in the buckram and prevents its weave pattern from showing through the fashion fabric.

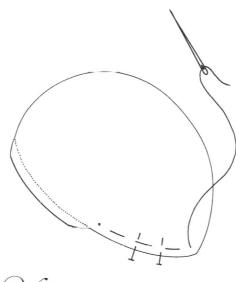

WORKING WITH THE BIAS

Look closely at any woven fabric and you will notice that it is made from threads that travel in two opposing directions. The threads running up and down — parallel to the tightly woven selvedge edge — constitute the straight grain of the fabric,

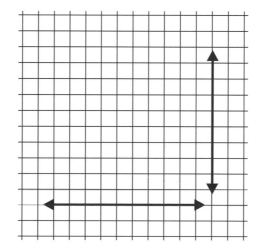

while the threads running side to side — perpendicular to the selvedge — are called the cross grain.

Try stretching the fabric in either of those directions, and you will find that it is nearly impossible, because the strength of the threads keeps the fabric stable.

Now try stretching the same piece of fabric at a 45-degree angle to those up-and-down and crosswise threads. Amazingly, this time the fabric will stretch. Congratulations! — You have just located the bias grain of the fabric.

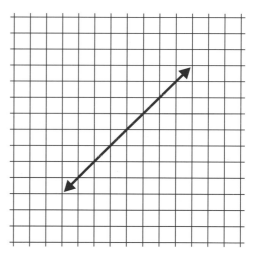

All bridal headpiece covering fabrics are cut on the bias. The "give" that you just experienced allows the fabrics to be fitted snugly and smoothly to the frame and to go around curves.

To locate your pattern's bias grain, crease the pattern vertically along the center line. Unfold it, then crease it again horizontally, bringing the bottom of the first fold up to meet the top. Unfold it again.

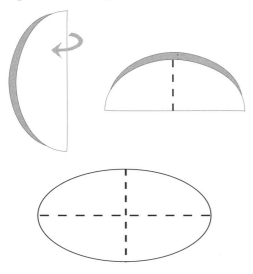

The two folds should now be crossing each other at a 90 degree angle resembling a crossroads. Turn the pattern piece if necessary so that the South road is shorter than its neighbors to the East and West. Crease the pattern piece a third time, at the intersection of the crossroads, bringing the bottom of the South road up and to the right to meet the East road.

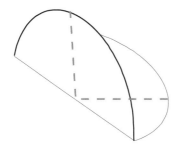

Unfold the pattern for the last time. The crease you just made bisects the crossroads at a 45 degree angle. Draw a pencil line along that crease and label it as your grain line.

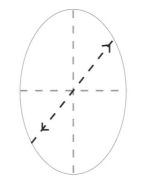

When cutting your fabrics, place this grain line along the *straight* grain of the fabric, parallel to the selvedge — This will put the center line of your pattern on the fabric's true bias.

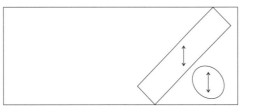

WHAT ABOUT LACE?

Lace has no true bias grain because it it not a woven fabric. Nevertheless, it is very flexible and should be easy to manipulate to lie flat on your headpiece. Cut the lace in any direction that allows the motifs to fall in a pleasing pattern on the headpiece.

SOMETIMES, YOU JUST CAN'T USE THE BIAS

If the design of your fabric dictates that it be cut on the straight grain rather than on the bias — for example, to center a brocade motif on the top of a pillbox hat — use the center line of each pattern piece as your straight grain marking.

It is still possible to achieve a good result with patterns cut on the straight grain of the fabric. Just take extra care to insure that the fabric lies flat against the frame, and adjust your seam allowances as needed.

SHOULD I SEW IT OR GLUE IT?

Try to assemble as much of your hat as possible using only a needle and thread. Sewing is strong, it can be done invisibly or nearly so, and best of all the stitches can be removed if the design or workmanship needs improvement.

Of course, there are some situations where a bottle of glue or a hot glue gun work best — The directions indicate where one of those techniques is most practical.

If you want to cover your hat using glue rather than sewing, that is certainly possible. Just be aware that "the point of no return" is reached every time you apply glue to a piece of fabric — Should you change your mind or make an error, you will probably have to start all over again.

The Pillbox Hat

Popularized in the early 1960's by Jacqueline Kennedy, a clean, tailored pillbox hat works well with a suit or a chicly simple sheath dress, while a pillbox piled high with lace, pearls and French veiling would be a magnificent finish for a heavily beaded satin ball gown or a mermaid silhouette.

You may wear your pillbox hat squarely on your head, tipped forward or back, or even placed at a jaunty angle off to one side.

MATERIALS

Buckram frame

1/2 yard each of fashion fabric, lining, and cotton flannel

3/4 yard narrow lace

Trimmings of your choice

MARKING THE CENTER OF YOUR FRAME

Turn the frame upside down and very gently squeeze in at the sides until the pressure causes the center front and the center back to become slightly pointed. Mark the front and back lightly with a pencil.

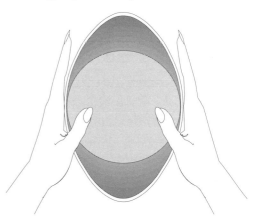

Transfer the center back and center front marks onto your patterns and to the wrong side of your fabrics as you cut them. Use the markings to position fabric pieces on the frame.

SHAPING THE FRAME TO FIT YOUR HEAD

Since your head resembles an oval rather than a circle, do not return the frame to its original round shape after locating the center. Instead, form it into an oval that feels comfortable and secure on your head.

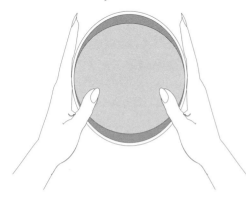

MAKE A PATTERN

Although the pillbox hat frame is pressed out of one piece of buckram, the covering and the lining are each made in two pieces: the top, called the lid, and the vertical section, called the sideband.

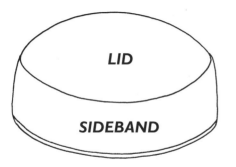

To make a pattern for the lid, turn your frame upside down on a piece of paper and trace around the outside edge.

For the sideband, start with a piece of paper about one and a half times longer than your hat's circumference and about three times wider than its height. Wrap the paper around the sideband, and fasten the two ends together with straight pins at the center back. Trace the top and bottom of the sideband, as well as the center back seam, onto the paper.

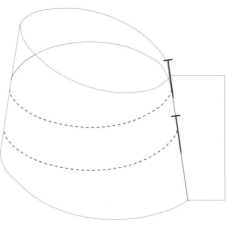

Make three individual sets of patterns

FASHION FABRIC

Add 5/8" seam allowance at the top and bottom of the sideband and around the edge of the lid, and 1/4" at the center back seam.

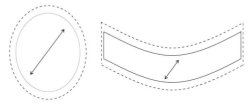

LINING

Add 5/8" seam allowance at the top and bottom of the sideband, 3/8" around the edge of the lid, and nothing at the center back seam.

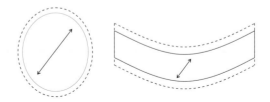

FLANNEL

Add 5/8" seam allowance at the bottom of the sideband, 1/4" around the edge of the lid, and nothing at the center back.

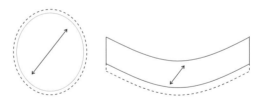

Cut one piece each in fabric, flannel, and lining — all on the bias.

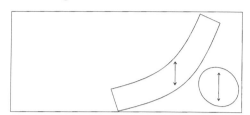

If you need help working with the bias, turn back to page 89.

NOTE

Because of the "give" of the bias, the seam allowances that you added to the pattern pieces will not always be the same as the seam allowances that you will be using as you assemble your hat. Don't worry too much about what that means — Just follow the directions carefully and you'll be fine!

𝒯LANNEL COVERING

Center the flannel on the frame's lid and baste it to the buckram. Trim away the excess seam allowance.

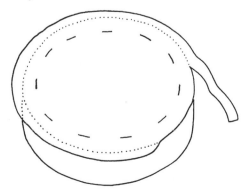

Center the flannel sideband on the center front of your frame, with almost all of the excess hanging below the bottom of the frame. Smooth the flannel toward the back, and trim it so that it just meets at the center back.

Stitch both ends of the flannel to the frame near the bottom. Stitch the center back edges of the flannel together, working your way toward the top but stopping about 1/2" from the top edge. Baste the flannel to the frame around the top of the sideband, about 1/2" from the edge.

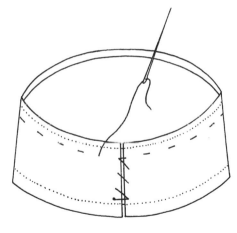

When you return to the center back, work your way back down to the bottom edge — It's easier and faster to just keep sewing than to knot and cut your thread and start all over again! Turn the seam allowance inside the hat and baste through the bottom of the frame just above the wire, catching all layers.

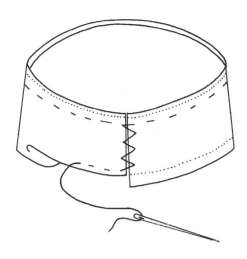

ℒINING

Assemble the lining by machine, using 5/8" seam allowances. Press the center back seam open, and press the seam allowance connecting the lid with the sideband toward the sideband. Use a pressing ham if you have one, as shown.

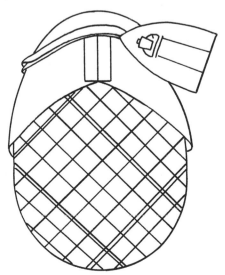

Place the assembled lining inside the hat frame. If it appears to be too large or too small, adjust it now.

Working from the inside out, baste the lining to the frame all the way around the edge of the lid.

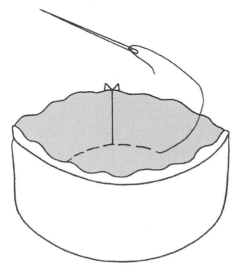

Pin the free edges of the lining up inside the frame to keep them temporarily out of your way as you complete the covering.

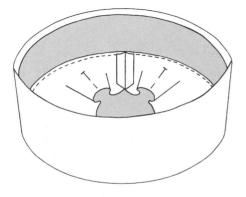

ABRIC COVERING

Clip into the seam allowance on the lid fabric every 1/2". The clips should be just 3/8" deep to insure they will not be visible on the finished hat. Baste the lid to the frame once through each clipped section.

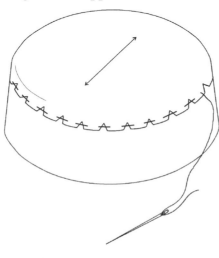

Sew the center back seam in the sideband fashion fabric, using a 5/8" seam allowance. Press the seam open and clip the seam allowances to 1/4" (Use pinking shears, if you have them). Slip the sideband onto the frame, keeping a seam allowance of about 1/2" at the top and letting the rest hang free at the bottom.

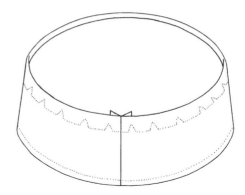

The sideband should fit snugly. If it seems loose, pin out the excess and resew the seam.

Turn under the seam allowance all the way around the lid. The edge that you form should be a soft roll, not a crease, and it should be even with the level of the lid.

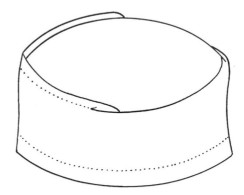

If the seam allowance shows through the fabric, push it underneath the flannel layer, so that the flannel lies flat between the seam allowance and the fabric.

At approximately two inch intervals, gently pull back the rolled edge and apply a teeny-tiny dot of white glue very close to the edge of the seam allowance only. This must be done

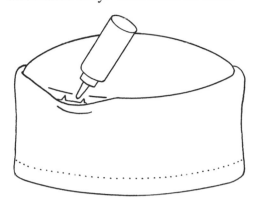

with complete precision — any glue that drips onto the body of the fabric will undoubtedly bleed through to the outside, and if the glue is too close to the rolled edge, it will squeeze out past the edge when you let go of it. If you wish, use a paintbrush to apply the glue rather than applying it directly from the squeeze bottle.

Fold the bottom seam allowance inside the hat. Remove the pins holding the lower edge of the lining to the lid, and turn the lining's seam allowance under so the edge lies just inside the hat. Pin as necessary, and sew the lining to the fashion fabric.

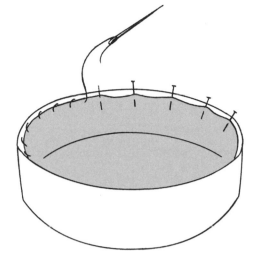

Finishing

Depending upon your hair style and the way you intend to wear your pillbox, you may prefer to have a comb at the front, back, or side of the hat. Sew a comb to the inside of the hat, or glue in a 4" length of elastic bridal loops and slip the comb's teeth through the loops.

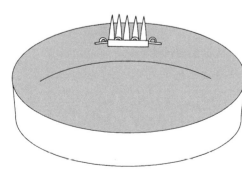

Sew your veil directly to the back of your pillbox hat, or sew a piece of

hook-and-loop tape there if your veil is going to be detachable.

For a Designer Touch, Add a Pleated Sideband

A sideband with three horizontal pleats is an elegantly tailored feature. Make each pleat from a separate bias strip and apply them individually.

Follow the assembly directions for a plain pillbox hat through the step where you have applied the fashion fabric lid to the frame.

Measure the height of the sideband and divide by three to determine the width of the pleats.

Cut three bias strips, each twice the pleat width plus 1" (If your pleats are 1/2" each, your bias strips will be 2" wide). Cut the strips exactly the length of the frame's circumference, adding no seam allowance so the bias-cut fabric will fit snugly over your frame.

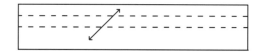

With right sides together, seam the short ends with a 1/4" seam allowance to make three individual loops of fabric. Press the seams open.

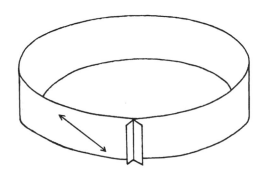

Fold the loops in half lengthwise so that one long edge is 1/4" below the other, and pin near the raw edges. The folds should be soft, not pressed in. These folded strips will form the individual pleats.

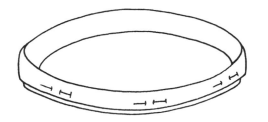

When positioning the pleats, place all of the seams at the center back unless a large flower or other trimming will cover them at one side. Apply each one with the longer edge toward the outside, and be sure to catch both layers in your stitches.

Place one pleat at the top of the sideband, arranging it evenly around the lid, and baste it to the frame.

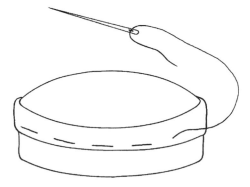

Baste the second pleat over the first so that its fold is 1/3 of the distance

between the bottom edge of the sideband and the top of the first pleat.

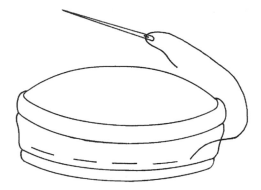

Place the third pleat over the second so that its fold is midway between the bottom edge of the sideband and the top of the second pleat.

Invisibly slip stitch the top of the pleat to the second one, so that it will stay in place after its seam allowance has been turned under the lower edge of the frame.

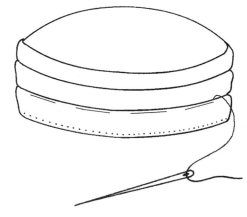

Fold the seam allowance inside the hat Tuck the lining's seam allowance under, so the edge lies just inside the hat.

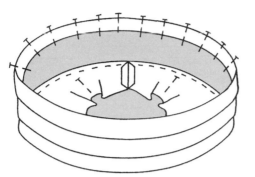

Remove the pins holding the lower edge of the lining to the lid, and turn the lining's seam allowance under so the edge lies just inside the hat. Pin as necessary, and sew the lining to the fashion fabric.

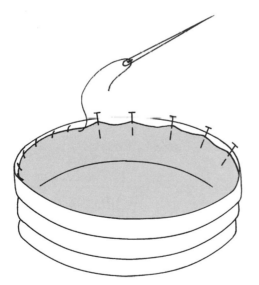

The Cocktail Hat

A sophisticated little round or tulip-shaped cocktail hat is gloriously chic when paired with a contemporary suit or minidress. Although it may have a standard veil of illusion, a cocktail hat is often accented with a bit of French veiling instead.

The cocktail hat shape is sometimes known as a tulip or petal frame, but is most often described as "that little round thing with kind of a point at one end". Variations include a heart shape and a perfectly round one like a skullcap.

MATERIALS

Buckram hat frame

1/4 yard each cotton flannel, fashion fabric, and lace lining

1/2 yard narrow lace

Trimmings of your choice

1/8 yard elastic bridal loops

Comb

Hook and loop tape

To make a pattern, trace around the outer edge, then add 1 1/2" - 2" all around for the fashion fabric, 1" for the flannel and the lining.

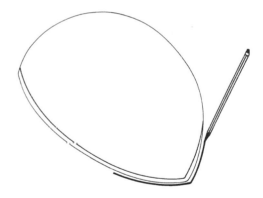

Cut one each — on the bias — in flannel, fashion fabric, and lining.

If you need help working with the bias, please review the directions on page 89.

FLANNEL COVERING

Center the flannel on the frame, and pin it evenly all around. Take advantage of the flannel's bias give to stretch it smoothly over the top of the frame and ease it in evenly around the edges.

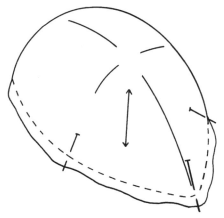

Stitch the flannel by hand or by machine to the edge of the frame just inside the wire. Clip the seam allowance to 1/4".

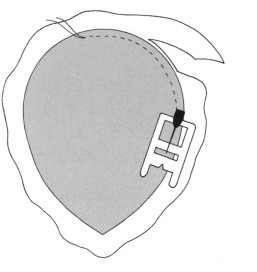

CHOOSING A FABRIC COVERING STYLE

Depending upon your design, you may decide to give your cocktail hat a perfectly smooth covering or to pleat a section of your fabric as you ease it over the frame.

The pleated covering is a bit easier, particularly for a beginning milliner. If you like, you can hide the pleats under a pouf or a cluster of flowers or other trimmings.

A SMOOTH FABRIC COVERING

Pin your fashion fabric to the edge of the frame, easing it along the bias as you did the flannel. If your head-piece design includes an edging — lace, pearls, etc — around the hat that will hide the stitches, sew through the right side, the frame, and the turned

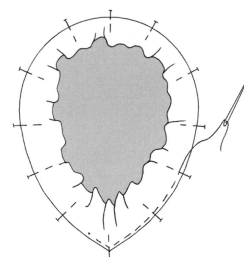

under edge. Do this step by hand so your machine's mechanism cannot mar your fashion fabric. If there is not an edging around the hat, pin under the seam allowance and hot glue it to the inside of the frame. Clip away the excess seam allowance.

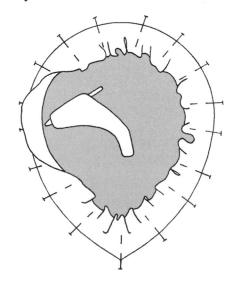

A PLEATED COVERING

If you wish to focus attention toward the back of your hat, pin the fashion fabric smoothly to the front of the frame and push the remaining fabric toward the back. Keep the fabric smooth until you are within about 1 1/2" - 2" of the center back marking.

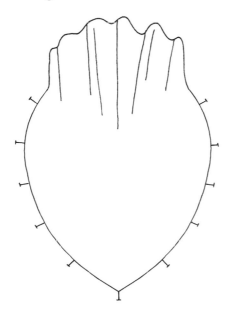

Form small pleats from the excess fabric, facing them toward the center back.

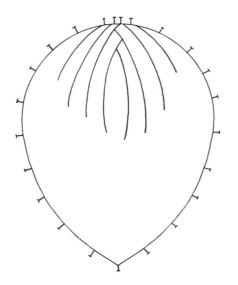

Use the same technique to gather the fabric to one side, if that is the focal point of your design.

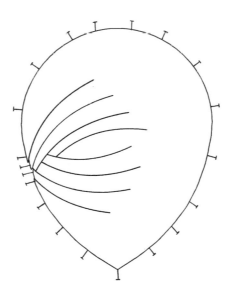

ℒINING

Hot glue the center of the lining to the top inside of the frame to keep it from falling out of the hat.

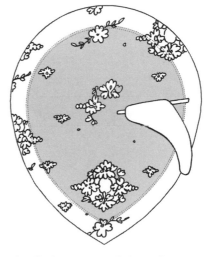

Pin the lining around the edges and hot glue it to the seam allowance of the fashion fabric, gluing right through the lace to the fabric. Clip

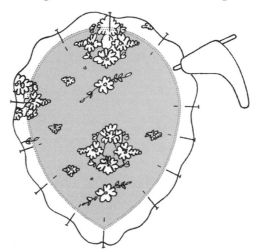

away the excess and hot glue a narrow (1/4" - 3/8") edging lace over the raw edge of the lining.

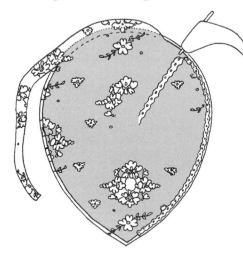

𝓕INISHING

Sew a comb to the inside of the back of the cocktail hat, or glue a 4" length of elastic bridal loops to the lining and slip the comb's teeth through the loops.

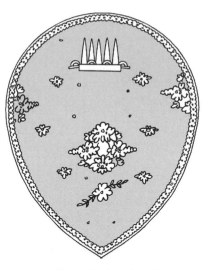

Sew your veil to the back of the hat, or a piece of hook-and-loop tape if your veil is to be detachable.

You can use these same techniques to cover any small buckram hat frame.

𝒯he 𝒫icture 𝓗at

At the turn of the century, ladies were so fond of "having their picture made" — meaning either a painted portrait or a photograph — in these elaborate wide-brimmed hats, that they became known as Picture Hats.

Picture hats are perfect for a garden or Victorian wedding. For a Scarlett O'Hara "Gone With the Wind" look, wear your picture hat with a full-skirted ball gown. A slender bride can accentuate her columnar Audrey Hepburn look with a close-fitting sheath dress topped by a very wide-brimmed hat.

Pay careful attention to your propor-

tions and the shape of your gown when considering a picture hat. The hat will add some height, and you can appear to be drowning under it if it is too large. A picture hat draws attention upward, so be sure your gown can balance that effect.

MATERIALS

Satin-covered buckram frame

1 1/2 yards fashion fabric

1/2 yard lining fabric

Trimmings of your choice

1/4 yard elastic bridal loops

Comb

Hook and loop tape

Purchase a semi-finished satin frame for your picture hat. Flannel is too heavy and bulky to make a suitable interlining for such a large hat — It would make the hat look and feel oversized and clumsy.

COVERING YOUR HAT

A picture hat has two sections, the crown and the brim. There are several becoming ways to cover each of the two sections.

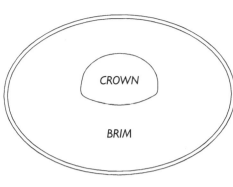

Cut all fabrics for your picture hat covering on the bias. If you need help working with the bias, please turn to page 89.

A PLEATED OR GATHERED BRIM

This is the easiest way to cover a brim.

To make a pattern, trace around the outside and the inside of the brim. Measure the width of the brim, then

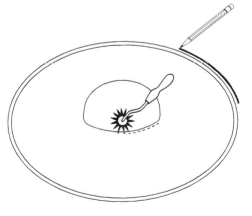

add that amount plus a 1" seam allowance all around the outside tracing. Add 1" seam allowance at the inside of the brim.

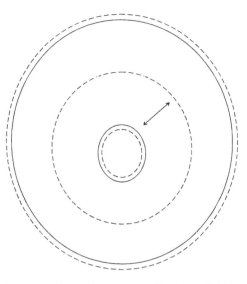

Cut one piece from your fashion fabric.

If the covering is to be gathered, run two rows of gathering stitches around the outside of the fabric about 1/2" and 3/4" from the edge. Clip the inner seam allowance at 1" intervals.

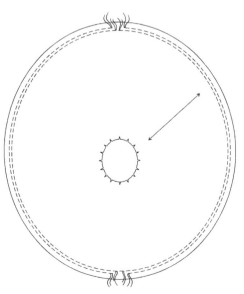

Baste the seam allowance to the inside of the crown.

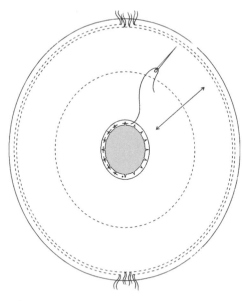

Bring the outside edge of the fabric up and over the top of the brim. Baste the edge to the crown, adjusting the gathers or pleating in the excess fabric.

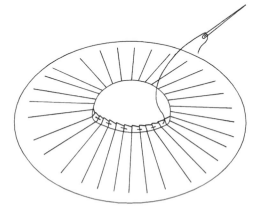

A SMOOTH BRIM

To make a pattern, trace around the outside and the inside of the brim.

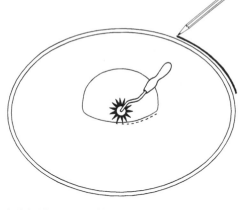

Add 1" seam allowance at both the outside and the inside edges.

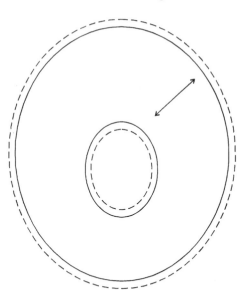

Cut two pieces in fashion fabric. Clip the inner seam allowance at 1" intervals. Position one piece of fabric over the top of the brim, and baste the inner seam allowance to the crown. Sew it by hand or by machine to the edge of the brim just inside the wire, and trim the seam allowance to 1/4".

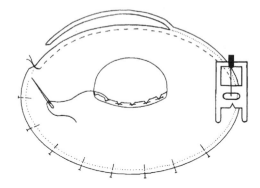

Turn the hat upside down and position the second piece of fashion fabric over the brim. Baste the seam allowance to the inside of the hat.

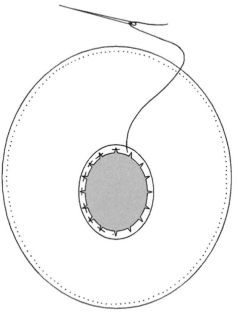

Turn the hat right side up and bring the outer edges of the fabric up and around the edge of the brim. Hot glue the fabric in place close to the edge and cut off the excess seam allowance. Cover the raw edge with lace, pearls, or a bias strip of the same fabric.

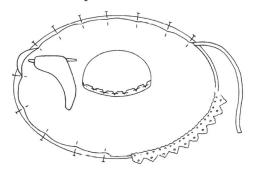

You can reverse either of these techniques to make the underside of the brim your focal point Make the choice based on the overall design of your hat, the placement of trimmings, and your hairstyle — If your hairstyle is a simple one, the added detail underneath the brim can be a lovely frame for your fashion, but if your hair style is more elaborate, the trimmings may confuse your total look rather than enhancing it.

AN EVENLY GATHERED OR PLEATED CROWN

To make a pattern, measure across the top of the crown from back to front and from side to side. Draw an

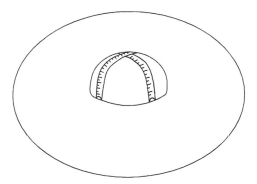

oval using those measurements. No seam allowance is added because the edge of the fabric should not extend below the base of the crown.

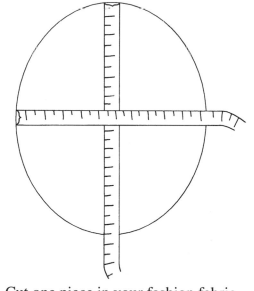

Cut one piece in your fashion fabric. For a gathered covering, run two

rows of gathering stitches about 3/8" and 5/8" from the edge.

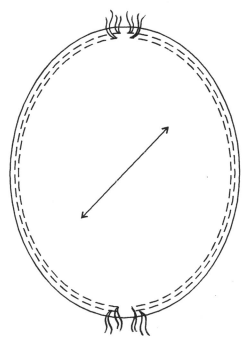

Center the covering over the crown. Draw up the gathering threads evenly and baste the covering to the frame.

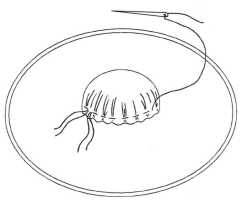

For a more tailored look, pleat the edge of your covering to fit the frame.

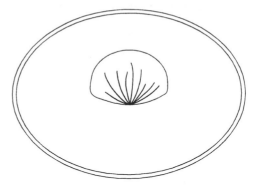

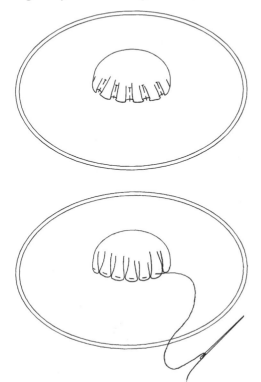

A DRAPED CROWN

To make a pattern, draw a right triangle that measures 27" on two sides. The bias occurs on the long third side of the triangle.

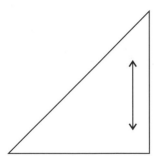

Cut one piece in your fashion fabric.

Pin the center of the bias side of the triangle to the center front. Stretch and pin the point of the triangle opposite the center front to the center back. Stretch the bias edge slightly while smoothing it toward the back, and bring the two sides of the fabric together at the center back.

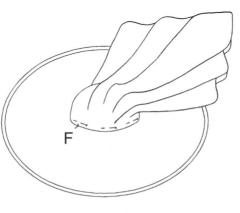

F

Arrange all of the excess fabric into pleats radiating toward the center back.

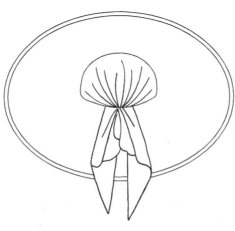

Baste the covering to the crown, and cut away the excess fabric.

If your trimmings are concentrated to one side of your picture hat, you may locate your pleats on that side instead of at the back.

*L*INING

Cut a rectangle on the straight grain from lining fabric that is 7" wide and 24" long.

With right sides together, seam the two short ends, using a 5/8" seam allowance. Press the seam open.

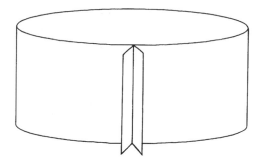

Turning under the edge 1/2" as you sew, run a row of gathering threads by hand or by machine close to one edge.

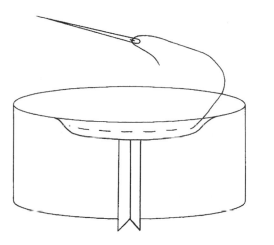

Turn under the other edge 1/2" and sew it to the fashion fabric at the inside of the crown, matching center backs and easing in any excess.

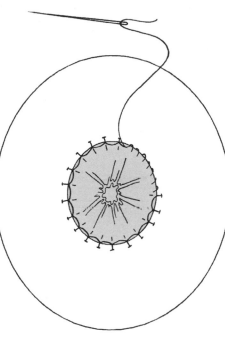

Draw up the gathering threads at the center until the lining fits the inside of the crown. Knot the threads and hot glue the lining to the top of the hat just inside the gathering. Cover the opening at the center with a lace applique.

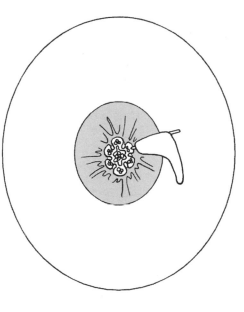

A SQUARE CROWN

If your hat's crown is flat on top rather than rounded, cover and line it as described in the directions for a pillbox hat on page 91. Turn under the raw edges at the bottom of the sideband.

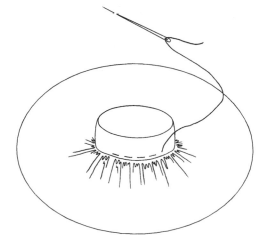

FINISHING

Cover the raw edges at the base of your crown with lace, flowers, ribbon, pearls, or a bias-cut band of the same or contrasting fabric.

Depending upon your hair style and the way you intend to wear your picture hat, you may prefer to have a comb at the front or at the back of the hat. Sew a comb to the inside of the hat, or glue a 4" length of elastic bridal loops to the lining and slip the comb's teeth through the loops.

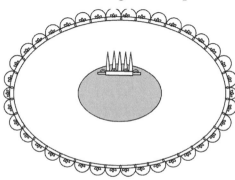

Sew your veil to the back of your picture hat, substituting a length of hook and loop tape if your veil will be detachable.

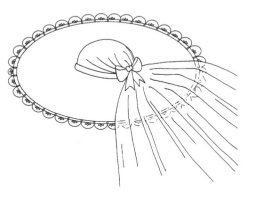

A Horsehair Picture Hat

A picture hat made of horsehair braid is light in weight and naturally translucent. It doesn't really require

a covering — You can trim it just as it comes. Add a hat band in fabric to

match your gown, or simply glue lace appliques to the crown and the brim for a more formal wedding.

If you do want to cover your horsehair hat, use a lightweight, sheer fabric, like organza, chiffon, or lace. Only the crown and the top of the brim are covered, so the hat remains translucent and does not become too heavy.

MATERIALS

Purchased horsehair hat

Lace appliques

OR

1 1/2 yards lightweight fashion fabric

1 1/2 yards millinery wire

1/8 yard elastic bridal loops

Comb

Hook and loop tape

Trimmings of your choice

FABRIC COVERING

Sew a length of millinery wire around the brim with a zigzag stitch about 3/4" from the edge. The wire will keep the brim from drooping under its own weight, and will allow you to bend it and shape it as you wish.

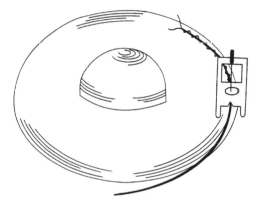

To make a pattern for the brim, trace around the outside and the inside of

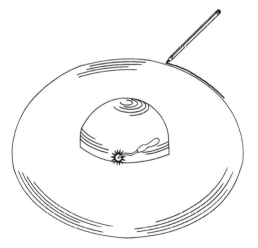

the brim. Cut just one layer of fashion fabric — on the bias — with a seam allowance of 1" at the center and 1/4" around the outside.

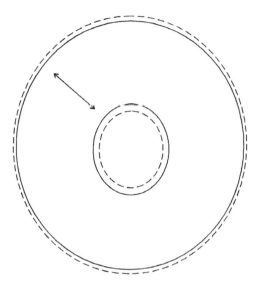

If your need assistance in working with the bias, please turn to page 89.

If your need assistance in working with the bias, please turn to page 89.

Finish the outside edge of the fabric with a serger or a zigzag stitch, and apply a lace or ruffled edging if you wish. Clip the inside seam allowance and baste the covering to the bottom of the crown.

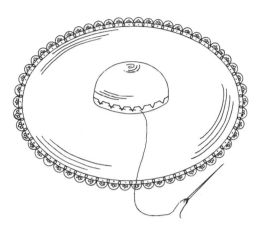

Cover the crown using one of the two methods described in the section on covering a buckram picture hat frame. Hide the raw edges at the base of the crown with a hat band of ribbon or a bias-cut length of fabric.

Sew a comb to the inside of the hat, or glue in a 4" length of elastic bridal loops and slip the comb's teeth through the loops.

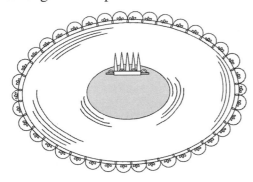

Sew a piece of hook and loop tape to the back of your picture hat if your veil is to be detachable. Or, you can sew your veil directly to the hat.

Altering a Buckram Hat Frame

If you cannot locate a buckram frame for the hat design that you have in mind, try altering an existing frame. You can easily shorten a pillbox frame, narrow a picture hat brim all around or just at the front, or cut the entire outer edge into a scalloped or geometric pattern.

To alter a frame, remove the binding and wire from the edge. To release the chain stitch holding the binding and wire to the frame, remove the thread from the last loop and pull — The entire row of

stitching should be released with that one tug.

Cut your buckram frame to the desired shape. Straighten out the wire as much as possible (see page 8), and replace the wire and binding by hand or by machine.

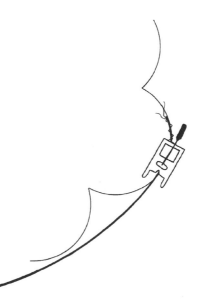

POTPOURRI

Congratulations! — You've just designed and made your own unique bridal headpiece, with exquisite professional results. Now you've nothing left to do but sit back, relax, and practice sounding humble as you prepare to answer the compliments you'll receive with a bride-like and demure "Thank you, I made it myself!"

This final chapter of "I DO" VEILS gives you all the information you need to keep your headpiece securely fastened to your head throughout your entire wedding day, and tells you how to preserve your headpiece as a family heirloom. The Resources Directory lets you in on the purchasing secrets of the professional milliners — Being able to put your hands on the right supplies and trimmings is half the battle, and most of the fun!

And — now that you've seen how easy it is — perhaps you'd like to make a few special headpieces for your bridesmaids and flower girls to wear as well.

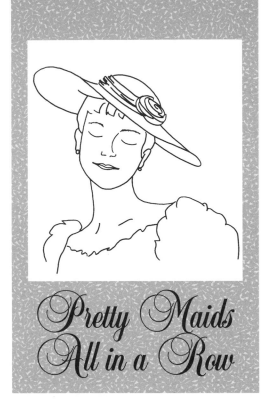

Pretty Maids All in a Row

Once you and your bridesmaids have settled upon a design for their dresses, it is wise to schedule another shopping day for everyone to get together and try on headpieces, so that you can choose a headpiece style that looks great on everyone.

To receive courteous service, don't announce to the salon salespeople that you're there looking for designs to copy yourselves. But there's also no real reason to feel guilty about it — If the salon is able to show you the perfect headpieces at the perfect price, it's possible that you would decide to purchase them there rather than making

them — It's really up to the salesperson to turn your "spy mission" into a sale!

What Style Will Look Fabulous on All of My Bridesmaids?

Just as your bridesmaids' dresses were selected to flatter even the most difficult-to-fit girl in the wedding party, keep the bridesmaids' hair styles and lengths in mind when choosing their headpieces.

It is a fact of wedding life that medium length to long hair is easier to deal with when selecting headpieces for the bridesmaids. A very short straight hairstyle cannot hold a barrette or a comb without looking downright silly, nor can short hair be swept away from the face and held at the back of the head with a cluster of flowers.

For a harmonious total picture that is not confusing to look at, every bridesmaid in the wedding party should wear the identical headpiece in the identical way. If even one bridesmaid wears her hair short and straight, consider hats for the entire wedding party instead of barrettes or combs.

If the group is diverse enough that no one choice seems right for everyone, bear in mind that the wedding police

will NOT arrive to break up the reception if the girls are wearing no headpieces at all.

The design for the bridesmaids' headpieces might incorporate a detail or trimming from their own dresses or from the bride's gown. They could be a smaller, more colorful version of what the bride is wearing. The bridesmaids' headpieces should never be larger than the bride's headpiece, unless they are wearing hats and she is not.

A decorated barrette, comb, or banana clip is easy to wear and is weightless enough to last through the entire reception. Compose a delicate arrangement of silk or handmade flowers, and add lily of the valley sprays to hang down or pearl sprays to stand up or away. Use a single larger flower instead for a dramatic effect, or a combination of stones and crystal beads for a dazzling yet simple elegance.

Picture hats seem to fall in and out of popularity for bridesmaids, but they are always appropriate for an outdoor summer wedding. Horsehair hats are available in a wide array of colors, and are easy to customize with fabrics and trimmings to match the bridesmaids' dresses. Straw hats are lovely for an informal or Victorian wedding.

A pillbox, cocktail hat, or other hat shape that flatters the bridesmaids and complements their dresses is suitable wedding attire. Keep the design simple, though, or these hats may easily steal focus from the bride.

Juliet caps, headbands, and wreaths can also make lovely and unusual headpieces for the bridesmaids. If it suits the style of the wedding, a short veil — 18" or less — of maline or tulle can be attached with hook and loop tape to allow it to be removed after the ceremony.

JUNIOR BRIDESMAIDS

If the dresses are identical or nearly so, a junior bridesmaid's headpiece is usually a smaller version of what the bridesmaids are wearing.

If the junior bridesmaid is very young, design her headpiece as a bridge between the styles of the bridesmaids and the flower girls.

ꜰLOWER GIRLS

Headpieces for flower girls are ruled by a completely different set of guidelines. The choice of headpiece style should be made based upon the style of the wedding and the personality of the child herself — her age, maturity, and her hair style.

The only hard and fast rule of thumb? — The flower girl's headpiece should have "Oh, how sweet!" written all over it.

Flower wreaths are the most popular flower girl headpieces, because a

wreath is most likely to stay in place on a fidgety head of silky-fine hair.

If the child and her hair style can handle it, a barrette or comb at the crest of the head will hold the hair nicely away from her face. A decorated headband or banana clip are also good choices, especially if the child is used to those types of hair accessories anyway — They are less likely to be pulled off at the first opportunity, and should remain in place at least until the main photographs have been taken.

The flower girl's headpiece may simply be a smaller version of what the bridesmaids are wearing, as long as the style is not too sophisticated.

A small-scaled hat of straw or horsehair is winsome and adorable, while a tiny beaded tiara lends a kind of tongue-in-cheek sophistication that reminds

us that the entire wedding party is really playing at dress-up for the day.

ᴀ TRIP TO THE SALON

The bride almost always has her hair styled at a salon for the wedding — Why not consider the same pampering for the bridesmaids and flower girls? An hour or two of "female bonding", particularly if the ceremony is an afternoon or evening affair, reduces stress and may be the wedding party's only opportunity that day for quality time with the bride.

On the practical side, gathering the entire wedding party in one location at the same time will help to insure that the bridesmaids' hair styles all have a similar feel and are all compatible with the headpieces. The stylist can even position and secure the headpieces on each bridesmaid, or at least show them how to do it themselves later.

You may find it more convenient to ask your hair stylist to come to your home on the day of your wedding to style everyone's hair. Be sure to have a special space with a large mirror set aside for the purpose — a spacious bathroom, dressing room, or bedroom would be ideal.

Wearing Your Headpiece

Nearly every bride is subject to a few stress-induced pre-wedding nightmares. A classic scenario involves that panicky moment when you are walking down the aisle and suddenly you feel your headpiece begin to succumb to its own weight and slide slowly but surely down the back of your head until it lies in a limp puddle behind you. Bridesmaids and groomsmen trip over the veil and in domino fashion the entire wedding party falls to the ground.

Not a great way to begin a marriage! Luckily, the alarm goes off and you are rescued from your nightmare, but

somehow the memory lingers, haunting you until the reception has ended and your headpiece has been tossed casually onto a bedside chair.

Breathtaking as a headpiece may be, it will only look fabulous as long as it remains on your head. A headpiece that has been trampled by bridesmaids, flower girls, and assorted aunts and uncles has very little chance of staying in one piece, much less being properly repositioned by well-meaning amateurs without a mirror or a clue.

Fortunately, you can relax and put aside this particular nightmare — With a few simple tricks, even the finest hair and the straightest hairstyle can support a headpiece.

"BUT THE COMB WON'T STAY IN MY HAIR!"

If you never expected to have much in common with actresses, ballerinas, or Vegas showgirls, now is your chance! What you are about to learn is an old theatrical trick, passed down through generations of wardrobe, hair, and makeup artists.

Very few women have hair with enough body to hold a comb unassisted. Even if your hair is sufficiently thick, coarse, and curly the weight of your headpiece, the movement of your head, and the overzealous hugs of all your new in-laws will eventually pull your headpiece free.

The comb's teeth must be given something to "bite into" that is stronger than hair. Metal is stronger than hair, so a pin curl held in place with a couple of metal bobby pins will effectively stop the comb from sliding out of position.

Form a pin curl at the exact location where you want the comb to adhere: Take a strand of hair at least 1/2" in diameter and saturate it with a hair styling gel. Twist the strand as you wind it loosely around one finger. Push the spiral of hair down the finger until it rests flat against the head. Hold the pin curl in place with two crossed bobby pins.

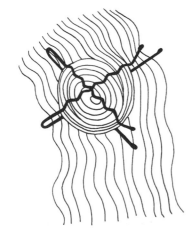

When you are satisfied that the pin curl itself is secure, position the

comb over it and push the comb's teeth under the bobby pins. The headpiece is not going anywhere.

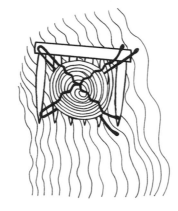

More CHEAP THEATRICS!

Solving the problem at hand quickly and effectively often requires conjuring up an unexpected and unorthodox solution. Be creative, and don't be timid about using whatever crazy tricks you've got up your sleeve to keep your headpiece in place.

TAMING A SLIPPERY HAT OR HEADPIECE

Apply self-adhesive foam carpet tape (available at hardware stores) to the inside of a barrette or picture hat. The foam tape grips your hair and helps to keep the hat or headpiece stationary on your head.

MANTILLA MAGIC

Use snaps to keep a mantilla draped artistically around your shoulders.

Because of its unique circular cut, a mantilla may tend to collapse in on itself at the center back, so cheat a bit by invisibly securing it to either shoulder with tiny clear plastic snaps, or snaps covered with fabric to blend with your gown. The snaps should be tiny and weak enough that the slightest tug will loosen the snap rather than tearing the veil.

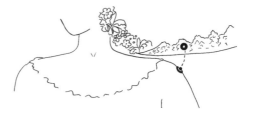

HORSEHAIR LOOPS

If your headpiece is large or heavy, use horsehair braid to make loops, then sew or glue them to the inside of your headpiece. Use the horsehair loops to invisibly bobby-pin your headpiece to your hair. To make horsehair loops, follow the directions given on page 13.

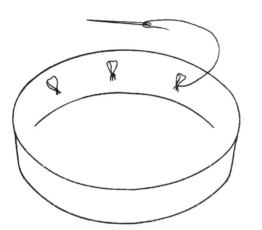

Care & Preservation

Even if it is never worn by another bride, a headpiece is a tangible wedding memento valuable to your family's cultural history. A sturdily constructed headpiece should last well beyond its one glorious day in the spotlight, conceivably still holding together mightily after twenty, fifty, or even one hundred years.

To maintain its shape and structural integrity, store your headpiece separately from your wedding gown in an acid-free environment. It is important to protect your headpiece from its natural enemies: dirt, light, moisture, and contact with other garments.

To prevent the headpiece or any other heirloom garment from being eaten away by the very storage system designed to protect it, always use acid-free boxes and tissue paper. Residual acids used in the manufacture of other papers will weaken, discolor, and eventually disintegrate the materials.

Some acid-free boxes and papers are buffered with calcium carbonate, an alkali that eventually destroys protein fibers. If your headpiece includes any silk or wool, be sure to order only non-buffered acid free boxes and paper.

You may wish to do some minor restoration before storing the headpiece, replacing a missing pearl or a frayed flower. Attempts to clean makeup or soil from a headpiece will likely do more harm than good — The stains may smear, discoloring the fabric or trims, and if your frame is made of buckram it will surely wilt. If your veil is detachable and none of its trimmings have been glued on, it can be dry cleaned, but the illusion will lose most of its body.

Make a support for the body of your headpiece so that it does not become crushed by its own weight during storage. The ideal foundation is a styrofoam head (or just the top of one —

slice the foam with a turkey carving knife). Cover it in tissue paper or washed muslin torn from an old cotton sheet. Alternatively, stuff the headpiece with pads of crumpled tissue paper or polyfill covered in muslin or tissue.

Glue blocks of covered foam or acid-free cardboard to the sides of the acid-free box in positions that will keep the headpiece upright and immobile. Place your headpiece in the box, isolating it as much as possible from the veil, and surround it with more crumpled tissue paper.

Fold your veil softly, with tissue paper layered between each fold, and arrange it loosely around the headpiece. If your veil is detachable, store it separately, also folded in tissue.

Place the box in a dark, dry closet or under a bed. Basements and attics are completely unsuitable for storing any heirloom garments — A basement's dampness causes mildew and attracts insects, both of which will quickly destroy the materials, while the radical temperature changes in an attic weaken the fibers. To shield the box from dust, cover it with muslin sheeting. Never use plastic, as it traps moisture that could damage your headpiece.

Given a headpiece's natural fragility, doing your best to protect it properly is your only hope that it will remain intact through years of storage. Even so, be aware that your best may simply not be good enough — Glues and fibers all naturally break down over time, and a stored headpiece may require restoration at a later date.

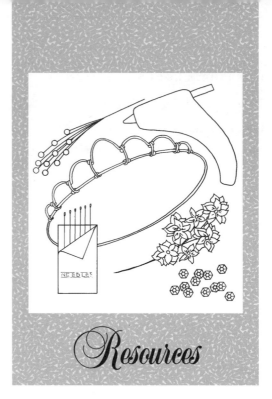

Resources

For anyone involved in the sewing or craft fields, the prospect of a new resource creates an excitement that can only be compared to Christmas morning. A new supply catalog that arrives in the mail is a surprise just waiting for its manilla gift wrapping to be torn off and its contents explored.

USING THE DIRECTORY

Wouldn't it be fantastic if every single thing you wanted and needed were available from one resource? Unfortunately, it doesn't work that way. Each supplier has certain niche items that are better than anyone else's or are simply unavailable elsewhere. The best way to shop is to determine which resources can supply you with what you need, then build a minimum order around those items. It may be expensive at the beginning to deal with more than one supplier, but it really is true that you can never have too many flowers, frames, and trimmings. Having plenty to work with right at your fingertips will provide inspiration for more headpiece designs than you could ever hope to complete.

Resources listed in this section have mail order departments proven to be speedy and reliable. Unless otherwise noted, all have catalogs available.

WHOLESALE PURCHASING

This directory lists both wholesale and retail mail order sources.

Professionals engaged in the manufacture of bridal headpieces can and should be purchasing components and This does not apply only to major manufacturers and retail bridal shops — Individual bridal dressmakers doing just a few weddings a month are legally considered manufacturers, and you can increase your profits by purchasing at wholesale as well.

Purchasing at wholesale requires a state vendor's license with a tax exempt resale number. Some sources

further require that your order or catalog request be written on your company's letterhead stationery or be accompanied by a business card.

Retail customers will not be able to purchase from wholesalers in this directory. Some suppliers, however, sell at both wholesale and retail, with two separate price lists and different minimum requirements.

RESOURCE DIRECTORY

B. B. WORLD CORPORATION

2200 South Maple Avenue
Los Angeles, California 90011
Phone: (213) 748-9990
            1-800-742-5557
Fax: (213) 748-6900

Wholesale only

Minimum order: $250.00. For smaller orders, there is a surcharge of $10.00 (Worth it!).

The mother lode of bridal flowers at unbelievably low prices. Unique items unavailable elsewhere. Also pearls, pearl sprays, pre-made veils and poufs, accessories, pearl bands, crowns, a few frames and finished headpieces.

BANASCH'S

2810 Highland Avenue
Cincinnati Ohio 45212
Phone: (513) 731-2040
Fax: (513) 731-2090

Wholesale and Retail

Minimum Order: $25.00

Sewing and workroom supplies, including silk hand sewing thread.

BEAD DIFFERENT

214 East Chicago Avenue
Westmont, Illinois 60559
Phone: (708) 323-1962
Fax: (708) 323-5529

Retail

No minimum order

A reliable retail source for stock trimmings, sequins, pearls and beads.

CATAN FLORAL COMPANY

17647 Foltz Industrial Parkway
Strongsville, Ohio 44136
Phone: (216) 572-9946
            1-800-782-3012
Fax: (216) 572-9954

Wholesale only (Catan's operates a number of retail craft stores in the Cleveland, Ohio area, but no retail mail order)

Minimum order: $75.00

A good basic selection of flowers and components at very low prices — pearls, pearl sprays, leaves, trims, and bands, pre-made veils, some frames.

CINDERELLA

60 West 38th Street
New York, New York 10018
Phone: (212) 840-0644
Fax: (212) 398-6458

Wholesale and retail

Minimum order: $30.00

A great selection of components available for retail purchase. No minimum quantities, but prices get better as the quantities increase. Wire, flowers, feathers, laces, Austrian crystal beads, sequins, pearls, horsehair, illusion, frames, finished headpieces.

SIDNEY COE, INC.

State Highway 36 East
Airport Plaza
Hazlet, New Jersey 07730
Phone: (908) 739-1168
Fax: (908) 739-0980

Wholesale and retail

Minimum order: None

The best source for fine quality pearls and Austrian crystals at excellent prices. Also beads and sequins.

GREENBERG & HAMMER, INC.

24 West 57th Street
New York New York 10019
Phone: (212) 246-2835/2836
Fax: (212) 765-5135

Retail

Minimum Order: $10.00

Retail supplier of notions and workroom supplies, including wire, buckram, and milliners' needles.

HYMAN HENDLER AND SONS, INC.

729 East Temple Street
Los Angeles, California 90012
Phone: (800) 421- 8963
Fax: (213) 617-1440

Wholesale and Retail

Minimum Order: $35.00

Known the world over for their unique imported ribbons. A good source for matching a particular lace. Hendler's also carries fabrics, trimmings, frames, beads, and sequins.

THE JAY COMPANY

150 Croton Avenue
Peekskill, New York 10566
Phone: (914) 736-0600
Fax: (914) 736-0936

Wholesale only

Minimum order: No specific dollar amount, quantities vary.

An unusual assortment of flowers and ribbon colors. They have rattail in a true pale ivory, which is very hard to find (often rattail called ivory has a yellow-green cast). Also, pearl sprays and other trimmings.

LIGHT IMPRESSIONS

439 Monroe Avenue
P. O. Box 940
Rochester, New York 14603
Phone: (800) 828-6216
Fax: (800) 828-5539

Wholesale and retail.

No Minimum Order

Acid-free boxes and tissue paper. An affordable "Heirloom Fabric Box Kit" includes a box (17" x 29" x 6"), tissue, dessicant, and plastic bags.

**MANNY'S MILLINERY
SUPPLY CENTER**

26 West 38th Street
New York, New York 10018
Phone: (212) 840-2235/2236
Fax: (212) 944-0178

Wholesale and retail.

Minimum order: $25.00

A fantastic selection of supplies and components at great prices. No minimum quantities — buy one hat frame or a dozen, one yard of illusion or a bolt. Manny's has it all — wire, frames, flowers, ribbons, horsehair, trims, finished hats.

**MILLINERS SUPPLY
COMPANY, INC.**

911 Elm Street
Dallas, Texas 75202
Phone: (214) 742-8284
Fax: (214) 742-8020

Wholesale and retail

Minimum Order: $30.00

A complete selection of frames and workroom supplies. Austrian crystal beads, laces, French veiling (they call it Russian veiling), flowers, feathers, pearls, pearl sprays, wire, crowns, pre-made veils and poufs, illusion, maline.

C. M. OFFRAY & SON, INC.

41 Madison Avenue
New York, New York 10010
Phone: (212) 213-4285
Fax: (212) 213-6158

Wholesale Only

Minimum Order: $25.00

Extensive selection of all kinds of ribbons at excellent wholesale prices.

PREMIER SYDELL

30 Crossways East
Bohemia, New York 11716
Phone: (516) 567-7450
        1-800-645-5750
Fax: (516) 567-7597

Wholesale only

Minimum Order: $250.00

The only importer of wired rouleau. They sell mainly to wholesale florists, not individual retailers or manufacturers. Call them for a wholesale florist in your area, where you might also find other items from their line of unusual components.

SPOSABELLA LACE

252 West 40th Street
New York, New York 10018
Phone: (212) 354-4729
Fax: (212) 944-9142

Wholesale and Retail

No minimum order

Lace edgings and yardage, finished headpieces. The largest selection of lace in the country. Send them a magazine photo of a gown and they will match the lace exactly for you. Prices are NOT bargain basement, but they do have everything.

STEINLAUF AND STOLLER

239 West 39th Street
New York, New York 10018
Phone: (212) 869-0321
Fax: (212) 302-4465

Wholesale and retail. No catalog.

Minimum Order: $30.00

Workroom supplies, wire, buckram, and the very nicest millinery needles.

UNIVERSITY PRODUCTS, INC.

517 Main Street
P. O. Box 101
Holyoke, Massachussetts 01041
Phone: (800) 628-1912
       (Orders only)
       (800) 762-1165
       (Information)
Fax: (800) 532-9281

Wholesale and Retail

No minimum order

Acid-free boxes and tissue paper. An archival hat box, 13-1/2" square by 12-1/2" deep, or a large textile storage box, 30" x 18" x 6" would be perfect for storing a single bridal headpiece and veil. Both are affordable.

WASHINGTON MILLINERY

P. O. Box 5718
Derwood, Maryland 20855
Phone: (301) 963-4444
       1-800-368-2753
Fax: (301) 963-8402

Wholesale and retail

Minimum order: $50.00

Their color catalog is as close as you might come to one-stop shopping. Wire and supplies, flowers, frames, pearls, pearl sprays, leaves, trims, and bands, frames, lace, buckram, French veiling, illusion, accessories, finished headpieces.

INDEX